ADVANCE PRAISE FOR
MASTERING SELF-DISCIPLINE

In *Mastering Self-Discipline*, Brinig presents an intelligent approach to conquering the difficult challenge of self-discipline in our everyday lives. Unlike the brute-force technique of just trying harder, he places self-discipline in the context of principle-based living, making its exercise much easier than it otherwise is. His book presents unique and workable strategies to increase effectiveness in your personal and professional life.

—*Josh Linkner, Innovation Expert,
Tech Entrepreneur and Bestselling Author*

Brinig's book, *Mastering Self-Discipline*, presents a lifelong map to achieving goals and success in your life. Each of our lives takes us on a long journey with many crossroads. This book provides the reader with a toolbox of ideas, concepts and processes that will help us decide which road to take in order to make us the best that we can be.

—*D. Paul Regan, Past Chair of California Society of Certified Public Accountants, former Mayor of Hillsborough, California, and Managing Principal of Hemming Morse, LLP, CPAs*

Brian Peter Brinig has transitioned his professional research from finance and economics to the skill of personal discipline. The strategies, visions and goals he identifies and clearly explains in *Mastering Self-Discipline* are truly insightful. The application of those principles makes controlling our personal and professional lives much more meaningful, productive and efficient.

>   —*Marc D. Adelman, trial attorney, past president State Bar of California, certified specialist legal malpractice law*

Mastering Self-Discipline outlines a broad, thoughtful strategy for applying the rigors of self-discipline to your daily living. It is a fresh look at a difficult subject that challenges all of us in our daily lives. Brinig's techniques will assist you on your road to success.

>   —*Jay E. Fishman, FASA, founder and Managing Director of Financial Research Associates, author of four acclaimed technical books*

Do you ever have the feeling you are leaving "success money" on the table because you haven't been as effective as you know you could be? Don't feel alone. In *Mastering Self-Discipline*, Brian Brinig offers a road map for us all to gain that extra bit of traction in life. One of the most useful ideas in *Mastering Self-Discipline* is that of the "next hour." Brinig asks us to focus on what we are doing in the moment, or in the next hour of our lives—in light of what we know we need to do. I've found this a helpful reminder to focus on that which is important in my life. I promise you will benefit if you read *Mastering Self-Discipline: A Thoughtful Approach*—and take action!

>   —*Z. Christopher Mercer, FASA, CFA, CEO Mercer Capital, Memphis, Tennessee, author and speaker*

MASTERING
SELF-DISCIPLINE

A THOUGHTFUL APPROACH
GETS BETTER RESULTS

BRIAN PETER BRINIG, JD, CPA

BURLINGTON BUSINESS PRESS

Copyright © 2020 Brian Peter Brinig

ALL RIGHTS RESERVED
No part of this book may be translated, used, or reproduced in any form or by any means, in whole or in part, electronic or mechanical, including photocopying, recording, taping, or by any information storage or retrieval system without express written permission from the author or the publisher, except for the use in brief quotations within critical articles and reviews.

(www.brianbrinig.com +brian@brianbrinig.com)

Limits of Liability and Disclaimer of Warranty:
The authors and/or publisher shall not be liable for your misuse of this material. The contents are strictly for informational and educational purposes only.

Warning—Disclaimer:
The purpose of this book is to educate and entertain. The authors and/or publisher do not guarantee that anyone following these techniques, suggestions, tips, ideas, or strategies will become successful. The author and/or publisher shall have neither liability nor responsibility to anyone with respect to any loss or damage caused, or alleged to be caused, directly or indirectly by the information contained in this book. Further, readers should be aware that Internet websites listed in this work may have changed or disappeared between when this work was written and when it is read.

Published by Burlington Business Press
New York – Palo Alto – San Diego

Printed and bound in the United States of America
ISBN (paperback): 978-0-578-61337-6
ISBN (hardback): 978-0-578-62714-4

Library of Congress Control Number: 2019920583

TABLE OF CONTENTS

SECTION I – INTRODUCTION

1. Introduction 1
2. Why You Should Care 9

SECTION II – THE FOUNDATION OF SELF-DISCIPLINE

3. Finding Your Soul 17
4. Determining Your Core Values 21
5. Creating a Vision for Your Life 37
6. What Is Your Life Purpose? 49
7. Developing Your Guiding Principles 53
8. The Importance of Alignment 69

SECTION III – PLAN OF ACTION FOR SELF-DISCIPLINE

9. Integrity of Commitment 77
10. Understanding and Establishing Goals 81
11. Making Goals Actionable: Tasking and Time-Adjusting 95

SECTION IV – PLAN OF EXECUTION FOR SELF-DISCIPLINE

12. Strategies for Self-Discipline 107

Alignment

Integrity of Commitment

Effort

Understand Your Strengths and Weaknesses

Know Your Personality

Make Yourself Proud

Attitude

Live in the Present

Happiness Is Now

Disproportionate Belief in Your Capabilities

Compare Yourself to a Standard

Fantasizing versus Planning

Constant Reward

Guilt

Controlling Your Mindset Is Easier Than Controlling Your Body

Controlling Your Destiny

Developing the Habit of Self-Discipline

The Desire for Constant Self-Improvement

Use Past Success as a Basis for New Frontiers

The Character Trait of Self-Denial

13. Tactics for Task Accomplishment 129
    General Tactics 132
    Daily Tactics 145

SECTION V – ROADBLOCKS TO SELF-DISCIPLINE

14. The Seven Deadly Sins of Task Avoidance ...163
15. Procrastination 173

SECTION VI – LIVING A DISCIPLINED LIFE

16. Self-Discipline Is Leadership: The Character, Cohesion and Direction of the Group 181
17. The Results of Self-Discipline 187

APPENDIX: Self-Discipline Tool Kit 189

ABOUT THE AUTHOR 191

SECTION I
INTRODUCTION

CHAPTER 1

INTRODUCTION

In the ninth week of Marine Corps boot camp, each platoon of recruits is assigned to mess hall duty, the job of providing support to the different eating facilities on Parris Island, the infamous Marine Corps Recruit Depot off the coast of South Carolina. Even though recruits are assigned the lowest-level jobs working in the mess hall, that week's duty is a welcome break from the intense physical routine of basic training.

A few days before mess hall duty, Gunnery Sergeant J. L. Smith, the senior drill instructor, screamed out different assignments to groups of recruits in my platoon. There was kitchen support (peeling potatoes, cracking thousands of eggs), dishwashing duties, cleanup duties, warehouse stocking, and outside policing of the grounds. Gunny Smith shouted out one more assignment: "Brinig, you're in charge of the GI shed!" I thought to myself, "What the hell's a GI shed?" I had no idea, but I soon learned that the GI shed was the mess hall's garbage room hidden deep inside the core of the building.

It's only after spending eight weeks in the living hell of Marine Corps boot camp, in the sweltering heat of a South Carolina summer, being relentlessly harassed for sixteen hours a day, that being assigned to the garbage room on mess hall duty is a relief. The GI shed, so named as a slur to the disrespected Army, is a smelly but *air-conditioned* 12' × 12' room where barrels of sloppy garbage are poured onto screen grates for hand-sorting by recruits to extract milk cartons and discarded silverware before the residue is sold to local pig farmers. Heaven on earth was a dark, smelly, air-conditioned room where no one of higher rank dared to enter because of the stench. Here, I was free from the terrors of boot camp for an entire week. I was in heaven.

How did I end up delighted with a garbage-sorting assignment that summer? My father was chief of surgery at a 300-bed hospital, and my mother's family operated a major business in my community. My older brother was attending Georgetown University, and 98 percent of my high school class went off to college after graduation. But I was happy picking through garbage in a dark, stench-filled room.

I ranked 316th out of 324 in my all-boys Catholic high school in Erie, Pennsylvania. I just didn't see the point of English literature and algebra II. I was much more interested in girls, sneaking cigarettes, and playing my guitar than reading Shakespeare. When I was in high school, no one had discovered attention deficit disorder, and there was only one explanation for my performance—laziness. That characterization didn't feel very good, and I didn't think it fit me very well, but it was the diagnosis of my poor life performance up to that point. I got no credit for being personable, being able to throw a baseball *and* play the guitar, or any other competence that didn't translate to a high SAT score.

Although both my parents and all my aunts and uncles were college educated, my poor high school performance led me to make the rounds of all the military recruiters in my senior year to see how I could "check the box" to complete a necessary evil of my generation: military service. I considered every option.

Why the Marines? A little-known fact of my time was that you couldn't just volunteer for the draft, which was a two-year enlist-

Chapter 1: Introduction

ment. You had to be nineteen years old to be voluntarily drafted, and I was young for my class, graduating from high school at seventeen and a half, so I didn't have the option of the draft and two years in the Army. All the other service branches had three- or four-year enlistments, some of which included reserve time after active duty. The Marine Corps was the only branch that had a two-year program. Even though I ranked 316th out of 324 in my class, I was smart enough to know that two years of misery was better than three or four, and all I had to do was figure out how to avoid getting shot as a two-year enlistee infantryman in the jungles of Vietnam.

It was dead silent on the Greyhound bus packed with sixty-four young men from every background imaginable as it wound its way through the darkness of the South Carolina coastlands. At 3:30 a.m., some were dozing and others pensively looked out the windows. I had heard rumors of what was about to happen, but I had no real idea how my life was about to change forever. Within the next hour, every familiarity with my previous life would instantly disintegrate as I was abruptly introduced to the most demanding of all military trainings, US Marine Corps basic training, commonly referred to as boot camp.

The bus entered the main gate of Parris Island, made its way to the intake barracks, and came to a halt at the edge of the parade grounds. An angry-looking staff sergeant with a Nicaragua campaign hat sprang up the steps of the bus and began screaming at us. "Swallow your gum! Sit up straight! Eyes straight ahead! When I say 'Get off the bus,' you fucking jump to attention and race down to the parade grounds and get your fucking asses on the footprints and don't fucking move!" I didn't know the "f-word" had so many descriptive qualities nor had I ever heard it inserted in the middle of any two- or three-syllable word, but I would soon learn that it could be, and often was. Everyone scrambled to stand at attention on the pre-painted footprints after we raced off the bus to the shouts of foul-mouthed drill instructors who seemed to multiply like rabbits. Soon there were eight or ten of them yelling at us.

In the first few hours of boot camp, everything was chaos. The noise level of the drill instructors was frightening and intimidating. Orders rang out. "Stand here! Go there! Do this! Do that!" Anyone with facial hair was ordered to go into the "head" and shave … of course, there was no shaving cream, only dull razors. Almost immediately, we were funneled into a room with five civilian barbers who were shaving heads to the shortest hair length possible, and not doing it gently. I recall seeing recruits with abrasions on their scalps from the barbers' electric shears. We were marched around to different barracks where we were photographed, fingerprinted, measured for clothing, and handed minimal toiletries. There was no sleep that night; this was the beginning of thirteen weeks of indoctrination into the United States Marine Corps.

I begin with this story because I *did* learn to master discipline as a young adult, but the technique I used won't work for most readers. As a seventeen-year-old private at Parris Island, I got all the discipline anyone would ever need. It was imposed on me by

Chapter 1: Introduction

my platoon's three loud, vulgar drill instructors who screamed orders at me from dawn until dusk and who had the authority to beat their recruits (and regularly did) if their orders were not precisely followed. For thirteen weeks in the sweltering South Carolina summer, I did more calisthenics than I ever dreamed could be done, force-marched more miles than I could imagine, and stood rigidly at attention for hours on end. From the moment I scrambled off the all-night bus and stood at attention on the painted footprints on the parade field, I developed a habit of externally enforced discipline that I have struggled to consistently achieve ever since, with limited success, I must confess. When your choice is "Do something … or else" and the "or else" is being slapped around by someone who has the power and authority to do it, an unruly seventeen-year-old kid gets religion pretty quickly. It doesn't take long to figure out that it's easier to stand at attention in the hot sun without flinching for an hour than it is to get smacked around and then sent to the worst possible fate of Marine Corps boot camp—Motivation Platoon. That's where the slackers were sent for a couple of days to learn how terrible their lives could be if they didn't get with the program. That wasn't going to be my fate; I got the religion.

I negotiated my twenties and early thirties with the help of my Marine Corps discipline, but I eventually lost the edge that had been honed at Parris Island. The discipline I developed in the military was externally enforced on me, but that model was not sustainable, although I could occasionally rely on my imaginary drill instructor to prod me along. I have been reasonably successful in both my professional and personal life, but I always felt I left too much on the field by not having the self-discipline to really "get at it" consistently. In my adulthood and professional career, there was nothing more frustrating than knowing what I should be doing but not having the consistent initiative (discipline, motivation, gumption, whatever) to do it. Only too well did I know the disappointment of not being able to discipline myself the way my drill instructors did. I spent years struggling with this demon, but I finally learned the secret to overcome it.

I undertook this study of self-discipline initially for myself and, because I am a teacher and a writer, I put my findings on these pages. My primary intention was to better understand the difficult task of exercising self-discipline in my adult life. We all know some people who seem to be able to do it all, at least in certain areas of their lives, and some of them even seem to have self-discipline in *every* area of their lives. Is there a secret? What is their secret? Is there a trick or tactic that makes exercising self-discipline easy, or at least easier? Are these self-discipline "machines" born or made? Where do their grit and determination come from? How do they make themselves "just do it" over and over? And most importantly, how could I learn to conquer this struggle?

Everyone wants to be better at self-discipline, the ability to more effectively force yourself to do the tasks necessary to advance your goals. It's both easy and hard. The easier part is understanding the foundation of self-discipline, because understanding is at the root of solving the challenge of self-discipline. The more difficult aspect is practicing self-discipline because of the effort required to do it, although there are many techniques to make the challenge easier.

The process of self-evaluation is foundational to mastering self-discipline. The exercise of self-discipline is based on a personal commitment to do the necessary tasks to achieve your goals. The basis of a strong personal commitment is the passionate desire to actualize your core values by achieving well-thought-out goals in alignment with those values. When I started the research for this book, I thought there was going to be a magic hack for the ease of self-discipline, but I have learned that the process is more complicated than employing a simple hack. There are many ways to make the application of self-discipline easier, but the process begins by developing a foundational basis for your goals before you get to the steps of implementing necessary tasks.

You *can* have more self-discipline; you just have to understand the context of a personal achievement process and where self-discipline fits into it. Then, there are strategies and tactics to make the seemingly overwhelming chore of exercising self-discipline easier. Don't get me wrong: I can't show you how to make it effortless, but you can learn to make it workable and incorporate it into your life. Understanding self-discipline in the larger context of our lives is critical to making its exercise easier. And surprisingly, if you learn to successfully integrate self-discipline into your life, your outlook and attitude will be much better than they otherwise would be.

The general concepts of self-discipline are similar in both a personal and professional setting, but their application in business is complicated by the fact that we're applying the concepts and techniques to a team rather than to an individual. In business, it is necessary to effectively communicate the components of a professional achievement plan to all the members of the group and seek commitment from everyone to the goals of the organization. The concepts, foundation, alignment, and implementation are substantially identical for mastering self-discipline in both life and business. If self-discipline is successfully integrated into the culture of a company, the team's positive outlook and attitude will create a professional environment that is much more conducive to collaboration, professional responsibility, growth and, ultimately, profitability. I have included Chapter 16, "Self-Discipline Is Leadership," to directly deal with the application of self-discipline concepts to the professional environment. There, I will highlight the minor differences between personal and professional self-discipline.

CHAPTER 2

WHY YOU SHOULD CARE

Why should you learn about self-discipline from me? In truth, I'm just another voice in the crowd, no smarter or better than anyone else. I am in the fourth quarter of my career, and as I review my progress, I am reasonably satisfied with how things have worked out. By any objective measure, I have been successful. But as I look back at my inefficiencies, I realize I could have been so much *more* successful if I had learned to master self-discipline earlier in my career. For me, it was always a fight—almost every day—trying to force myself to do difficult tasks and *somewhat* succeeding. Most people would say I have done pretty well, but it's frustrating that I could have done so much better if I'd known then what I know now.

There is definitely a solution to the art and science of mastering self-discipline. If you want to master something, you have to study it, learn everything about it, understand its components, and create a strategy that works for you in order to conquer it. In the pages that follow, I will introduce you to the larger context of principle-based living that forms the foundation necessary to embrace and have self-discipline in your life, both personally and professionally. Surprisingly, the need for self-discipline doesn't occur until the execution stage of a personal or professional achievement process, which is actually toward the end of the continuum, not at the beginning. We will study and understand the larger strategy of personal and professional achievement, and I will also include a number of self-discipline exercises that will help you to implement the tasks necessary to achieve your goals. For starters, here is the personal achievement process I continually refer to in this book:

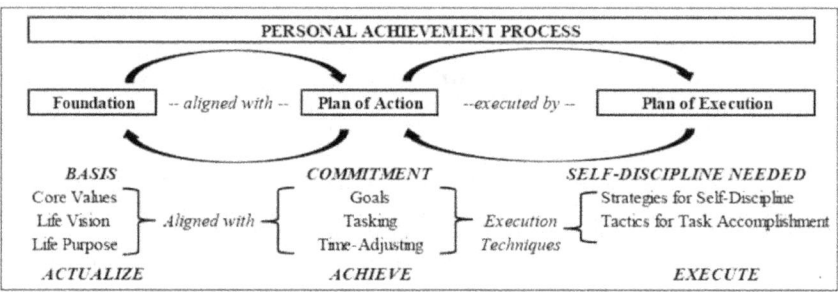

The personal achievement process is divided into three major categories: Foundation, Plan of Action and Plan of Execution. Each category consists of components that will be explained in subsequent chapters, but the process is a continuum of activity based on underlying principles that extends through the execution of necessary tasks to achieve goals. An early question to ask yourself is, do you really want to increase your self-discipline? You will learn the strategies and tactics of mastering self-discipline, and they're not particularly hard, but they *do* require personal effort to accomplish goals, and it may require a fundamental change in the way you approach your daily life.

You can force yourself to do almost anything in the short term. A college kid can pull an all-nighter and write the ten-page paper due tomorrow morning. An overweight person can starve himself for two days and lose a couple of pounds. You can force yourself to go to the gym and work up a sweat for an hour. These activities may appear to be self-discipline, and to a limited extent they are,

Chapter 2: Why You Should Care

but these activities are the exercise of discipline for a few minutes, or with a gun to your head. That is not *mastering* self-discipline. The "sugar high" of momentary, apparent self-discipline is great, and it may get you through a situation or two, but it won't take the place of learning self-discipline.

Remember, you *can* change. To quote Ralph Waldo Emerson, "The only person you are destined to become is the person you decide to be." Yes, read that sentence again: it means exactly what it says. You can be the person you want to be. Where you are in life is the accumulation of your habits. Are the habits you are living the ones you want to continue to make part of your life? Importantly, we must understand that habits can be changed, especially when we understand how they work.[1]

At one end of the self-discipline continuum we find a decorated former Navy Seal named Jocko Willink. He has written a book called *Discipline Equals Freedom*,[2] which is a short, interesting, and recommended read. I haven't had the pleasure of meeting Jocko yet, but from reading his book, he appears to be something of a fanatic[3] who screams at himself and beats himself up in order to be the most disciplined person on the planet. I got a little depressed reading his book (it took me about sixty minutes) because I concluded his technique just wasn't me and it was never going to be me. I can't simply yell at myself to go to the gym for three hours a day and promise never to eat another doughnut for the rest of my life, etc. But I did realize Jocko's method is just another approach to enforce self-discipline on oneself, and every method has some merit. Part of mastering self-discipline is learn-

---

1 Charles Duhigg, *The Power of Habit* (New York: Random House, 2012).
2 Jocko Willink, *Discipline Equals Freedom* (New York: St. Martin's Press, 2017).
3 I say this respectfully and, based on his book, I think Jocko would agree with my characterization.

ing you can be a better person without turning into Jocko, unless that's your style and that's who you want to be.

Somewhat similar to the "just force yourself" methodology of Willink's *Discipline Equals Freedom* is the Marine Corps drill instructor approach. If you put yourself in a situation where someone has the authority and power over you to force you to do things, you can acquire enough motivation to perform the necessary tasks to achieve your goals. I wouldn't call it self-discipline, but it is somebody's discipline over you that makes you perform, and it can get the job done, as impractical as that model may be. There are aspects of the drill instructor model worth considering, like a professional life coach who can help you structure your approach to achieving your goals.

At the other end of the spectrum is a more gentle, intellectual approach to the subject of self-discipline. I have had the great fortune to experience a wonderful ninety-seven-year-old woman named Deborah Szekely, the cofounder of the world-renowned fitness resort, Rancho La Puerta in Tecate, Mexico. In her weekly lecture to the attendees at "The Ranch," Deborah simply points out that every hour (or minute) of your life is a choice. You can choose to make the next hour of your life productive and advance your purpose in life, or not. You can choose to be the person you say you want to be for the next period of time, or the next ten push-ups, or the next hour of study, or not. You can really believe "this moment is my life" and you can make this moment self-enhancing or self-diminishing. Embarrassingly, it is just that simple. This thought brings me to the old adage, "If it is to be, it is up to me." Look at yourself in the mirror and repeat that saying about fifty times. There is no getting around it: you are responsible for your situation in life.

Chapter 2: Why You Should Care

One of the ways to make the difficult challenge of self-discipline easier is to expand your thinking to get into the mental framework of making self-enhancing tasks more tolerable. You don't have to do a hundred push-ups to be working toward getting in shape. Ten or fifteen will do the trick, but you *do* have to do them. You don't have to sit down and write a 20,000-word treatise; a few paragraphs in the next ten or fifteen minutes will move you in the right direction. Work on making less desirable tasks more desirable, but realize striving to achieve your goals won't be like eating cake at a birthday party. Use your creativity to make "work" easier and less offensive. There are ways to do it.

In the course of researching this book, I have changed myself. I have learned the basic job of mastering self-discipline begins with a character study and an understanding of the personal achievement process.[4] One of the keys is having a determined character, a purpose, a vision, and a commitment to being a better person. Yes, there are many tactics for implementing those principles, but the basic ingredient is having the determination and personal integrity to implement the tasks necessary to carry out the entire process.

Understanding there is no simple hack for self-discipline will keep you from wasting your time searching for it. I remember when I was in the ninth grade and many of us started cheating on tests in school, embarrassed as I am to admit it. We were preparing elaborate cheat sheets for the little quizzes our teachers were giving. Not only did I feel bad about cheating, but one day I came to the realization that if I spent as much time studying the course material as I spent trying to prepare an intricate cheat sheet, I

---

[4] All of the concepts and strategies of self-discipline also apply to our professional activities; the only difference is a team application of them. For individuals, I refer to a personal achievement process, and for business applications, a professional achievement process.

would pass the tests and maybe even learn something. Doing the right thing can initially seem harder than cutting a corner, but in the end, doing what one ought to be doing is the easiest road to success. And psychologically, knowing you are doing the right thing and are on your road to success is extremely beneficial to your overall well-being. The sooner you accept that reality, the better off you will be.

You *can* learn to be better at the art of self-discipline, and you can even elevate your understanding of the life strategy of discipline to a level of mastery. Knowledge is power, and learning about self-discipline is the beginning of changing this aspect of your life. Self-discipline is a core value; it is its own character trait that can be better understood and achieved. Just as kindness, integrity and morality are basic core values, so is the personal discipline required to make yourself do the necessary tasks to achieve your goals. My study of this subject has definitely made me a better person and enabled me to accomplish new goals I only dreamed about at the outset of this adventure.

SECTION II

THE FOUNDATION OF SELF-DISCIPLINE

CHAPTER 3

FINDING YOUR SOUL

Be the change you want to see in the world.
—Attributed to Mahatma Gandhi

Setting aside any religious philosophy, it's obvious there is more to our lives than whatever activity we are engaged in at the moment. Recognition of this fact is what separates humans from all other species and gives us a greater life purpose than just eating, sleeping, and enjoying ourselves in the moment. That greater purpose provides the foundation for choosing our destiny and ultimately mastering the control of our daily activities.

Merriam-Webster defines *soul* as "the immaterial essence, animating principle, or actuating cause of an individual life" and "the spiritual principle embodied in human beings ... or the universe."[5] Soul is also defined as "the spiritual or immaterial part of a human being ... and a person's moral or emotional nature of sense of identity."[6] One's soul incorporates all the mental abilities of a living being: reason, character, feeling, consciousness, memory, perception, thinking, etc.[7]

It is one thing to understand and acknowledge that human beings have souls, but we should all spend some time identifying

---

5 *Merriam-Webster*, s.v. "soul," https://www.merriam-webster.com/dictionary/soul.
6 *Lexico*, s.v. "soul," https://www.lexico.com/en/definition/soul. I make no apologies for footnoting non-authoritative sources if they provide well-crafted definitions or language.
7 Wikipedia, s.v. "soul," last modified October 14, 2019, https://en.wikipedia.org/wiki/Soul.

the components making up our souls. It is important to think about those components to understand our foundation. So often, we are on a path set by others—college is a great example—where our future is charted for us and we are cogs in the wheel of progress. Our vision is dictated to us, and we go through the motions of living to "check the boxes" that are put in front of us. If you are pleased with the path you are on, there's nothing wrong with having an externally imposed structure to help you achieve your goals. But this is an area where you have to be mindful of whether you are controlling your life or your life is controlling you. Defining your soul (your core values and your life vision) is the basis for everything you do and accomplish in your life.

It is critical to understand and accept that this foundation, this essence, this "soul," this Being, underlies everything we do. Importantly, each of us has the power to establish and shape our own Beings. So if you identify positive core values and a clear vision for yourself, that process will subconsciously establish the foundation for your actions and enable you to move forward thoughtfully in your life. Alternatively, if you don't choose to invest the time and energy to identify your values, you won't have a subconscious road map that's leading you to where you want to be. Inertia—or some vacuum of direction—will take over and you'll just be floundering, living from hour to hour and day to day without a meaningful purpose.

Interestingly, in the category of degrees of difficulty, it's not hard to establish core values and vision. It's like saying, "I'm going to be a good and worthwhile person." How hard is that? Candidly, it's a lot harder to *be* a good person than it is to *want* to be a good person, but you first have to want to be a good person. So here's one of the first self-discipline hacks: spend some time thinking about and establishing your core values and the vision for your life. That mental thought process, and a commitment to it, is foundational to getting you where you want to be. Character begins with having a solid basis of good core values and a positive, healthy vision for your life. Ultimately, it also includes the determination to execute and implement your core values.

CHAPTER 4

DETERMINING YOUR CORE VALUES:
WHAT DO YOU BELIEVE IN?

*I cannot find language of sufficient energy to convey
my sense of the sacredness of private integrity.*
—Ralph Waldo Emerson

Most of us reach adulthood with a set of core values imposed on us by our parents, teachers and the cultural institutions that formed our environment as we grew up. Everybody is a mixture of somethings: you are Jewish or Catholic or Muslim or agnostic; Republican or Democrat; politically interested or not; academic or sports minded or both or not; community oriented or withdrawn; or many other value-based characteristics. Our families brought us into their worlds and infused their belief systems in us and, in many cases, we are probably fine with those beliefs. But it is entirely possible you might have developed different beliefs as you matured.

Your core values are the canvas on which you paint your life. They are the underlying beliefs that are fundamental to your purpose for living. Your values are the compass of your life, giving you the basic direction for your conduct and activity. They are the things you believe are important in the way you live, love, interact with the world, and work. Your values have a major influence on your attitude and serve as broad, underlying behavioral guidelines in all situations in your life.

Part of the process of maturing involves understanding, choosing and committing to the core values that are presently important to you. Since the values that are significant to you may change over time, it is not surprising you might not be wedded to the ones your parents instilled in you as a child. But have you thought about your core values recently? Can you identify what current fundamental beliefs guide your life?

Your choice of values depends on your personality, your goals, and the mission you see for yourself (at least for the foreseeable future). Knowing and committing to your core values is the foundation for your success and prosperity, both personally and professionally. Without a set of values, it's as though you're trying to sail a ship through the ocean without a map or a plan. I suppose you could go out for a little weekend sail or scoot around the harbor from time to time, but without a map, you're not really going anywhere. Not having a set of values results in a completely unfocused life.

Aside from the aimlessness of trying to live a life without a clear set of core values, there is a very practical reason to commit to value-based living. Everyone is moving through life, doing something, trying to accomplish something. It is obvious any successful accomplishment requires a plan, and well-thought-out core values work as the foundation for your success. As you move into the implementation phase of your personal achievement process, when your actions match your values, you are satisfied and content. But when your actions don't align with your per-

Chapter 4: Determining Your Core Values: What Do You Believe In?

sonal values, things feel wrong. The best definition of happiness I have found is this: when you are doing things pursuant to and in alignment with your core values in life, you are happy. Right now. That's the only happiness we can have—happiness in the present. You can't feel an emotion tomorrow or yesterday; you can only experience it now. And, if you are acting pursuant to your core values and your beliefs, you are happy. Notice I am careful not to say you *will be* happy, I'm saying you *are* happy.

Humor me and try this for a few minutes. Take a few deep breaths and stop thinking about yesterday or tomorrow; bring yourself into the present. After a minute or two of relaxation, think about something you've been putting off from your to-do list—your good to-do list, not something nagging at you like cutting the grass or cleaning the garage, but some task pursuant to a worthy goal you have in the short term. As you think about this item on your list, think about breaking down the goal into smaller tasks. I promise you if you will spend thirty minutes pursuing one of those early, smaller tasks toward that goal, you will enjoy yourself and feel good and happy about working toward the goal. That's happiness—right here, right now. Seriously, take a break from reading sometime today and perform a task toward one of your worthwhile goals. See how it feels.

Core values and self-discipline are a bit of a "chicken and egg" problem. I am suggesting you need to go back to basics and focus on your core beliefs as the initial foundation for your success, the beginning of your mastery of self-discipline. In other words, you can't practically accomplish self-discipline if you don't have anything to be disciplined for. Ironically, the person you want to be and the person you are are pretty much the same. The sooner you realize that, the more grounded and successful you will be, and the more you will work to evolve into your vision of yourself.

In his 1989 book, *The Seven Habits of Highly Effective People*, Stephen Covey identifies immutable principles that are natural laws foundational to human growth and happiness. They are guidelines for human conduct that are proven to have enduring, permanent value. They're fundamental. They are essentially unarguable because they are self-evident. Covey's examples of immutable principles are fairness, integrity and honesty, human dignity, service, quality or excellence, potential, growth, patience, nurturance, encouragement, and living the Golden Rule. Covey points out that one way to quickly grasp the self-evident nature of these principles is to simply consider the absurdity of attempting to live an effective life based on their opposites. It is impossible to contemplate a quality life of deceit, deception, mistrust, and dishonesty. Without being religious, moralistic, or spiritual, let's accept the fact that these immutable principles, commonly referred to as "values," exist and should govern everyone's life. These are ethical values—the kinds of values having to do with being a kind, good person and doing the right thing in our interactions with others. These are indisputable principles of living. For those of us who want to have a quality, principle-centered life, these immutable principles are foundational. Here is a short list of them for you to contemplate and decide which ones are most important to you:

Honesty	Fairness
Integrity	Responsibility
Trustworthiness	Caring
Respect for Others	Compassion
The Golden Rule	Kindness

Chapter 4: Determining Your Core Values: What Do You Believe In?

Immutable principles are foundational laws governing human growth and happiness. Covey maintains that to the extent people live in harmony with these principles, they are moved toward survival and stability. I would suggest your determination of your personal core values should fit within the framework of immutable principles, but core values are personal beliefs and they can also incorporate some more selfish objectives without being contrary to immutable principles. Your core values should fit in with immutable principles, but they don't all have to be so good-hearted. There's nothing wrong with having some core values that are more self-centered, although they probably shouldn't be contradictory to Covey's immutable principles.

Core values are the fundamental beliefs in which you are emotionally invested (either for or against something). They are the very broad guidelines by which we all make decisions about what is more important or less important for us in pursuing our lives. Ultimately, your purpose in life is to realize and live your core values, and that objective is the very definition of being true to yourself.

It is important to understand core values, in and of themselves, are not right or wrong, good or bad. They are the basic beliefs, desires, and preferences for your life, and they determine what is important for you to do. We would hope a person's values are good and his actions are based on a set of moral and ethical principles, but for the limited purpose of understanding self-discipline, one's values are not assessed by any type of moral judgment of right or wrong. Core values determine what is important to a person, morals decide what is acceptable for him to do, and ethics govern the behavior of the person.

Sometimes one's core values are strengthened—for better or worse—by membership in a family or group sharing similar values, and they may even be enforced by rules of conduct that apply to the group. Examples would be religions, ethnic cultures, professional associations, schools or other groups that formally or informally subscribe to certain values and may have rules to enforce those values on their members. These institutional codes of conduct are generally beneficial to provide foundations for our lives. For instance, the core values of a West Point cadet would probably be quite clearly defined and significantly different from the values of a member of a Hare Krishna community. In each case, however, the successful individuals in the groups would subscribe to a set of core values that provide guidance and direction to their respective lives. Assuming one accepts the goals and purposes of the group are worthwhile, that person would agree that subscribing to the core values proposed by the group is a good thing.

Fundamentally, there are two categories of a person's core values: those values dealing with an individual's interactions with others, called "ethical" values (because they govern a person's behavior with the world), and values that are personal to the individual, called "non-ethical" values. The term "non-ethical" is an imperfect term because non-ethical values have nothing to do with ethics, morality or interactions with others; they are simply a person's individual beliefs about what is important to her for her private conduct. They are not unethical—they are simply non-ethical. Examples of these values would be beliefs that don't particularly affect other people; they are personal to the individual. Beliefs falling into this category would be values like constant self-improvement, health and fitness, profit motive or personal responsibility.

Chapter 4: Determining Your Core Values: What Do You Believe In?

An early step in the process of mastering self-discipline is reflecting on and determining your core values. You can change them as you move through life, but you should start with the understanding of what core values are and what the right ones are for you. Consider a menu of core values to guide you in understanding what yours might already be, or what new values you might want to add to your list. Here is a short list of ethical core values to consider; these are values that constitute a person's beliefs relating to her interactions with others:

"Ethical" Core Values

Carefulness	Generosity	Respect
Commitment	Gratitude	Responsibility
Compassion	Honesty	Service
Contribution	Integrity	Tolerance
Dependability	Justice	Trustworthiness
Empathy	Love	Truthfulness
Fidelity	Loyalty	Understanding

The other category of core values is referred to as non-ethical values, those which primarily affect you individually and don't directly relate to your relationship with others. These values can be more self-centered because you are the only one they pertain to. You have the right to pursue your non-ethical values to the point of negatively affecting others, and then your actions should be tempered to consider the consequences of your interactions (or lack of interactions) with others. Here is a short list of non-ethical values to consider:

"Non-Ethical" Core Values

Achievement	Growth	Professionalism
Competence	Happiness	Responsibility
Consistency	Health	Security
Creativity	Humility	Self-discipline
Decisiveness	Ingenuity	Self-reliance
Dignity	Mastery	Stability
Discipline	Moderation	Success
Enthusiasm	Motivation	Thoughtfulness
Excellence	Optimism	Traditionalism
Faith	Perseverance	Wealth
Gratitude	Persistence	Winning

A much longer list of ethical and non-ethical core values is presented at the end of this chapter for your consideration.

There is a process for determining the core values that are the most important ones to guide your life, and it begins with an honest evaluation of yourself. Contemplating your beliefs, your motivations, your desires and what is important to you is fundamental to choosing the core values that are intrinsic to your being. I suggest a two-pronged approach: first, simply review the long list of core values at the end of the chapter and take a first shot at picking five to ten from each sub-list (ethical and non-ethical) that initially feel relevant to you. That step will get you started in identifying your values. A deeper reflection about the beliefs that are most significant to you presently is also required. After some time spent on that question, you will choose core values that are the ideals you strive for to realize your purpose in life.

Reviewing the larger lists of core values enables you to reflect on values important to you. Ask yourself:

Chapter 4: Determining Your Core Values: What Do You Believe In?

1. What core beliefs are important to me in my interactions with others?
2. What core beliefs are important to me personally?

And continuing a self-evaluation, you can reflect on the following questions:

1. What motivates me, not in a superficial goal-oriented way, but in a deeply personal way?

    a. The desire to do good?
    b. Desire to accomplish X?
    c. Concern for others?
    d. Contribution to others?
    e. Concern for myself?
    f. Desire to please others?
    g. Desire to impress others?
    h. Desire to be respected?
    i. Desire to get things done?
    j. Desire to compete and win?
    k. Desire to be healthy?
    l. Desire to excel?
    m. Fear of failure?
    n. Hate to lose?
    o. Am I a person who wants to achieve something, or am I a person who wants to avoid something?

2. At the core of your being, what is important to you?

    a. Family?
    b. Relationships?
    c. Higher power?

d. Acceptance?
   e. Professional success?
   f. Helping others?
   g. Accomplishment?
   h. Health?
   i. Growth and development?
   j. Wealth?
   k. Power?

3. What characteristics do you see, or want to see, in yourself that please you?
   a. Compassion?
   b. Dependability?
   c. Honesty?
   d. Integrity?
   e. Loyalty?
   f. Responsibility?
   g. Trustworthiness?

4. What qualities in terms of dealing with others are important to you?
   a. Fairness?
   b. Dependability?
   c. Empathy?
   d. Generosity?
   e. Competing?
   f. Winning?

Think of your core values in a way that is inspiring to you, and understand that your chosen values will set your expectations. Once you have identified five to ten values that ring true for you, ask yourself if they encompass the most important aspects of the vision you have for yourself. Having core values only works if they're ideals and beliefs that are going to push you to excellence and hold you to high standards. Your prioritized core values must be a group of beliefs that are fundamentally right for you and that you will commit to as a foundation for your reason for existence.

To help you define the best core values at this point in your life, I suggest you reflect on times or activities that made you feel good, proud or fulfilled. The times you reflect on shouldn't be recreational or pleasure activities like a ski trip or a vacation; they need to be in the areas of personal or professional development. Activities involving family, development or educational and professional growth are good examples. Step back, look at the activity, and try to connect the motivations and objectives that underscored the activity to your feelings about accomplishing it. Ask yourself: "What was I doing?" and "Why was it so satisfying?" I suspect you will find the activity was closely connected to the deeper values and beliefs about what was important to you at that time.

Let me use school as an example for your reflection on a productive, "aligned" time in your life. It can be a great example of the connection between core values and one's willingness to be truly *engaged* in subsequent action, as opposed to just going along with the program. Assuming you were engaged in your educational path, what was the motivation for pursuing your education? Was it because you were committed to scholarship and education or was it simply because you wanted the degree? Or, was it because somebody else (like your parents) wanted you to get it? There's nothing wrong with any of these motivations, but think about the connection between the motivation (the core value, the belief) and the passion with which you undertook the necessary tasks to achieve the goal. If you deeply believed in the importance of the goal, your willingness to do the work to accomplish it was emotionally much easier than if you were doing it because somebody else wanted you to do it. There's nothing wrong if the only reason you went to college was to get the degree—that's okay, but that's a different motivation than the motivation of a person who's committed to lifelong education and intellectual development. And it's also different from the motivation (or lack thereof) created by someone else wanting you to do it. So, be careful—and truly introspective—when you're evaluating your historical motivations. For some folks, their motivation was simply to succeed at obtaining a degree, while others might have been pursuing intellectual growth. The third group might have been striving for something because it was important to someone else, and that isn't usually a great reason (motivation or core value) to do something.

So, what do you do with the result of this reflection? You ask yourself what motivations, needs and/or beliefs (core values) are currently valid for you. Now, they may be different from earlier values because as you go through life, your values will probably change. Your basic motivations and beliefs certainly change as your life situation changes, as you move from education, to family, to career, to retirement. Obviously, the core values of a twenty-one-year-old college student will be dramatically different from a sixty-year-old grandfather who is contemplating retirement in the next few years. For this reason alone, evaluating your core values is a lifelong exercise. The critical

Chapter 4: Determining Your Core Values: What Do You Believe In?

realization is the connection between the core values that are currently right for you and the action undertaken pursuant to those values. That connection is alignment, and it's what creates happiness and harmony in your life. In short, you're doing what you're supposed to be doing.

Knowing your real self is one of the keys to ultimately mastering self-discipline. It's infinitely easier to force yourself to do necessary tasks if they are aligned with your core values than it is to do tasks when you're fitting a square peg in a round hole (meaning you're out of alignment). The overall objective will ultimately be to figure out a way to make these necessary tasks more tolerable and even pleasant.

After you have selected ten to fifteen core values from the available lists (five to ten ethical and the same number from the non-ethical list), prioritize the list by determining which values are most important to you. Honestly, there is no magic to this step in the process, but it gives you the opportunity to contemplate these values in relation to your motivations and needs in life. Keeping in mind that core values are general beliefs setting a foundation for your conduct, be careful to choose values you are willing to commit to because you know they will have a significant impact on your personal and professional success. Don't be afraid to reaffirm your core values as you move through life. Do these values make you feel good about yourself? Are you proud of your values? Do these values represent things you would support, even if your choice isn't popular and it puts you in the minority? Be sure you are comfortable with positive answers to these questions.

For the benefit of your review and consideration, I offer the following incomplete lists of core values:

Mastering Self-Discipline

CORE VALUES - Ethical (E) and Non-ethical (N)

(N)	Accountability	(N)	Financial Responsibility	(N)	Prudence
(N)	Achievement			(E)	Reliability
(N)	Adventurousness	(N)	Fitness	(E)	Respect
(E)	Altruism	(N)	Fun	(N)	Responsibility
(N)	Ambition	(E)	Generosity	(N)	Resourcefulness
(N)	Balance	(N)	Grace	(N)	Restraint
(N)	Being the best	(E)	Gratitude	(N)	Results-oriented
(E)	Belonging	(N)	Growth	(N)	Rigor
(N)	Carefulness	(N)	Happiness	(N)	Security
(N)	Cheerfulness	(N)	Hard Work	(N)	Self-actualization
(N)	Commitment	(N)	Health	(N)	Self-control
(E)	Community	(N)	Holiness	(N)	Self-denial
(E)	Compassion	(E)	Honesty	(N)	Self-discipline
(N)	Competence	(E)	Honor	(N)	Selflessness
(N)	Competitiveness	(N)	Humility	(N)	Self-reliance
(N)	Consistency	(N)	Independence	(E)	Sensitivity
(N)	Contentment	(N)	Ingenuity	(N)	Serenity
(N)	Constant Improvement	(N)	Inner Harmony	(N)	Service
		(E)	Integrity	(N)	Simplicity
(N)	Contribution	(N)	Intelligence	(N)	Spontaneity
(N)	Control	(N)	Intellectual Status	(N)	Stability
(E)	Cooperation	(N)	Joy	(N)	Strength
(E)	Courtesy	(E)	Justice	(N)	Structure
(N)	Creativity	(E)	Leadership	(N)	Success
(N)	Curiosity	(E)	Love	(E)	Support
(N)	Decisiveness	(E)	Loyalty	(E)	Teamwork
(N)	Dependability	(N)	Making a difference	(N)	Temperance
(N)	Determination	(N)	Mastery	(N)	Thankfulness
(N)	Dignity	(N)	Moderation	(N)	Thoroughness

Chapter 4: Determining Your Core Values: What Do You Believe In?

(N)	Diligence	(N)	Motivation	(N)	Thoughtfulness
(N)	Discipline	(N)	Obedience	(N)	Thrifty
(N)	Dynamism	(N)	Openness	(N)	Timeliness
(N)	Economy	(N)	Optimism	(E)	Tolerance
(N)	Effectiveness	(N)	Order	(N)	Traditionalism
(N)	Efficiency	(N)	Patriotism	(E)	Trustworthiness
(N)	Elegance	(N)	Perfection	(N)	Truthfulness
(E)	Empathy	(N)	Perseverance	(E)	Understanding
(N)	Enjoyment	(N)	Persistence	(N)	Uniqueness
(N)	Enthusiasm	(N)	Piety	(E)	Unity
(N)	Excellence	(N)	Power	(N)	Usefulness
(E)	Fairness	(N)	Positivity	(N)	Vision
(N)	Faith	(N)	Practicality	(N)	Vitality
(E)	Family-oriented	(N)	Preparedness	(N)	Wealth
(E)	Fidelity	(N)	Professionalism	(N)	Winning

CHAPTER EXERCISE

1. Schedule a quiet time for personal reflection to review the list of core values.
2. Bring yourself into the present moment and contemplate who you fundamentally are and what you believe in.
3. Recognize your choice of core values depends on your fundamental beliefs, your personality, and the mission you see for your medium-term life.
4. Understand your choice of values will inform and significantly control the establishment of your goals.

5. Make a list of ten to fifteen core values that initially feel important to you, recognizing there may be many more that have some appeal to you.
6. Prioritize the list by contemplating which values are most important to you. Ultimately, you want to select the highest-priority four or five as the core values you primarily rely on.
7. It can be helpful to do this exercise with a close confidant and allow three to five minutes of continually responding to the same question, "What is most important to you?" You might be amazed at the result of paring the list down and reflectively digging deeper to determine the most important values in your life.
8. Remember that there is no perfect magic to choosing one's core values. It is simply a reflective process where you ask yourself what is important to you and what are your core beliefs.

CHAPTER 5

CREATING A VISION FOR YOUR LIFE

Vision is the art of seeing the invisible.
—Jonathan Swift

Every aspect of your life is on a trajectory. You are going somewhere, and the beauty of the ride is that you get to choose where. You can make it a good place, a neutral place, or a bad place. Some people don't care to choose—they just let life happen to them. However, the consensus among experts is that with a vision in mind, you are far more likely to succeed beyond what you could otherwise achieve. Think of crafting your life vision as mapping a path to your personal and professional dreams.

The concept of a life vision is both a trajectory for your near- and longer-term life plan as well as a static picture of your life at some point in the future. In creating a vision for yourself, it is important to develop a picture of yourself at a point in the future—not too far away—when you plan to have realized or completed some important goals.

You wouldn't be reading this book if you were the type of person who lets life happen to you. You have an innate desire to be a better person, to move forward and advance yourself. Your situation will not be stagnant—you know your life is a continuum, and you control the direction of the flow of events you experience. It's critically important to understand the dynamics of the path we are all on and use that understanding to take control of your destiny on this wonderful ride of our lives.

In this chapter, we pay attention to the path leading us to realize and actualize the core beliefs that make our lives important and worth living. If our lives are in a constant process of transformation, we can either be slaves to the changes of life or we can be masters of the evolutionary progression. Simply stated, how do we actualize and realize the core values we have now clearly defined for ourselves?

Creating a life vision is not a difficult process, but it takes time, energy, and the commitment to do it. Defining the path that makes you into the person you want to be can't be done in twenty minutes. You must consider what you want to accomplish, be known for, and whom you want to be surrounded by. What would your best life look like? What would it feel like? How will you feel when you are there? Your vision is the path you must identify and establish to take you to that place.

As you begin to create your vision, it's important to have a practical time frame in mind. If you're twenty years old, it's probably not immediately helpful to try to visualize your life at sixty-five. Consider dividing your vision into time periods you can relate to, realistic periods of your medium-term future life. It's a good idea to have a future life vision divided into identifiable time segments of from about three months to two or three years.

The power of having a clear vision for your life is immense. Clarity of vision sets up your subconscious mind for the success you visualize. We've all heard the expression, "As you think, you are." Well, think about it: you have the choice to visualize yourself

Chapter 5: Creating a Vision for Your Life

as a mediocre character, just shuffling along, or you can envision yourself as a happy, successful person, accomplished in your personal and professional relationships and thriving in your life. It's your choice.

As a freshman in college, I struggled with what I wanted to do with my professional career. As a teenager, I wanted to be an entrepreneur, a businessman like both my grandfathers. I also had some mentors who were in business, and I thought that would be a very rewarding thing to do. When I was in college, the dean of my business school was both a CPA and a lawyer. I had never heard of anyone with both those credentials, and I was impressed.

I started keeping a journal in 1970 when I was a freshman in college and I have maintained it, admittedly sporadically, ever since. When I was a sophomore in college, one day I wrote in my journal that I had decided "I am going to be a CPA lawyer. That would be a very cool thing to do, and that's what I am going to do." I didn't remember my visualization of this goal until about twelve years later when I went back and looked at the early entries in my journal and found the February 26, 1972, entry. I was licensed as a CPA in California in 1977 and I was sworn in as a member of the California Bar in November 1979. I achieved the vision I established as a college sophomore.

The compelling part of my story of achieving a goal through subconscious, creative visualization is after I imagined (and established) this goal for myself as a college sophomore, I couldn't have abandoned the goal with more fury. I couldn't have done more to directly sabotage the goal if I'd tried with every effort of my being. Yes, I graduated from Georgetown University with a degree in accounting and went to work at an international accounting firm. But I hated being an accountant so much I quit in disgust after twelve months and went to work as the manager of a tennis club, promising myself I would never again have anything to do with public accounting. Fortunately, I came to my senses and only managed the tennis club for about six months. After doing that and a couple of other things, I reluctantly decided to go to law school at age twenty-five because I didn't have anything better to do. When I got near the end of law school, I literally walked out of a big law firm where I was offered a job because everything I saw about the practice of law turned me off. I did graduate from law school (barely), but when it came time to take the bar exam, I was so dead set against it that I didn't initially register for it. But at the last minute I sent in a late fee and late-registered to take it. Fortunately—and by the grace of some higher power—I managed to pass the bar exam.

So, when I was thirty years old, I had gotten my CPA certificate and my license to practice law, even though I wasn't actively engaged in either of those professions at the time. I was a CPA lawyer ... pretty cool, I dare say. One day, I happened to go back to the journal I created when I was a freshman and sophomore in college and, to my utter shock, I found the entry that said "I'm going to be a CPA lawyer—that would be a cool thing to do." The irony of my achievement of this goal is if you had followed my progress year by year over those ten years, from the time I visualized the goal to the time I accomplished it, it's hard to think I could have done anything more to sabotage the goal. I walked out of a big-eight CPA firm I hated; I reluctantly went to law school and almost didn't take the bar exam; and I rejected the offer of a prestigious law firm because I couldn't see myself practicing law. How was it possible I became a CPA lawyer? It had to be that I created a vision for myself and my subconscious mind picked it up and almost forced me to accomplish the goal. Visualization works. Believe it and give it some effort.

You have gone through the thought process of developing and choosing your core values and you're committed to them, so you know what fundamental beliefs are important to you. With your selected core values as a backdrop, think of crafting your life vision as mapping a path to your personal and professional goals, with consideration of what characteristics you believe to be most important. You'll never live a life that matters until you define what matters, and defining what matters and your path to achieve it is the purpose of vision.

There are two steps to the visualization process: first, you create a static picture of your life at some point in the future, and second, you create a trajectory for your near- and medium-term life plan.

CREATING YOUR STATIC VISION

To develop a clear static vision for yourself, pick several points in time in the future—not too far away—when you plan to have realized or completed some important goal of yours. I suggest identifying three time periods to focus on, but engage in that mental exercise one period at a time. If there is no external reason to choose anything different, a thirty-day period, a six-month future date, and a three-year future date are good benchmarks. Obviously, if you have reason to choose other time periods, like a graduation or achieving some other milestone, those time frames are better for you. Just don't go twenty or thirty years into the future; that's too far away for the benefits of the visualization exercise.

In doing any of these mental exercises, it can be helpful to use mindfulness and meditative practices of relaxation and breathing techniques. There are numerous resources available to learn and practice meditation and, based on my research, a significant majority of successful people apply these techniques regularly. Don't ignore their benefits. At the very least, get comfortable with some basic relaxation techniques and use them for the purpose of visualizing your future self.

As an exercise in clarity of vision, take yourself to that place in the future and begin to be very specific about your surroundings. Focus on yourself at that place and time. Relax and calm yourself, removing any stress or worry from your mind. Pick the specific time period you are working on (thirty days, six months or the longer time) and explicitly identify your surroundings, whether you're outdoors or indoors, and other specific incidental factors contributing to the mental illustration or picture of the place. Now focus on the person in the vision, the future you who has accomplished the goal you are striving for. Try to feel that person, understanding the emotions present in the person who has accomplished that particular goal. How does your future self feel? How are you interacting with the people around you? Are you proud of your accomplishments and are those around you proud of you too? Don't rush this meditative exercise and don't hesitate to revisit it regularly as you work to visualize your success and create the subconscious reality that this vision is going to be you. Enjoy the feeling of your future success *now* and appreciate that you are setting a mental benchmark that vastly increases the probability of achieving your dream.

The visualization of a static point in the future of your success is an exercise you should do regularly because it will generate energy and enthusiasm to help strengthen your commitment to realize your core values. Creating your clear vision takes a commitment to your values and goals, and revisiting the visualization of yourself in the future regularly reinforces your commitment.

In the course of developing your vision, it can also be worthwhile to visualize the opposite of your dream. In order to contrast the positive feeling you imagine from accomplishing a quality vision for your life, visualize the failure to accomplish your vision and try to experience the feeling of that failure. During a time of quiet reflection, take yourself forward to a time in your life when your ideal vision should be completed and, instead of visualizing the successful accomplishment of your goals that are in alignment with your core values, visualize your life if you fail to accomplish those goals. What will it feel like if you don't achieve that professional success, or worse yet, if not only do you not achieve it, but you utterly fail at your objectives? Take a little time—not too long—to experience the disappointment of the failure to achieve your goals. What will it look like? What will it feel like? How will you interact with your friends and family if you don't accomplish your goals? This negative visualization of failure can be a worthwhile contrast to the positive visualization of success.

It is important to set lofty goals for ourselves. Setting a high goal for yourself means you might not perfectly accomplish the goal, but it is likely you will get to 70 percent or 80 percent or 90 percent of it. Don't be such a perfectionist that you consider achieving only 70 percent of your goal a failure, because that isn't failure. Abandoning your goal or not putting in a level of effort to try to achieve your goal could be viewed as failure, assuming your values and goals haven't changed. You *haven't* failed if you achieve a significant percentage of the high goal you set for yourself. In my professional practice as a consultant to business owners over the years of my career, I would always say, "You don't have to be perfect in your business decisions, only profitable." Achieving 70 percent or 80 percent of what you set out to do can certainly be appreciated as a success. Don't beat yourself up for not being perfect; just be "profitable."

CREATE A VISION OF THE PROCESS

The second aspect of creating a vision for your life is visualizing the *process* of achieving your ultimate goal (which is also your ultimate static vision). Since your goal (or goals) is thirty days to three years away, there will obviously be a number of steps that have to be accomplished to achieve the goal. Envisioning the process of achieving your goals definitely involves writing down the detailed steps to accomplish the goals (discussed in Chapters 10 and 11), but conceptually it involves contemplating the overview plan at the 10,000-foot level that will be used as a guideline to visualize the process of getting there. In this step, I'm not talking about focusing on the details of each interim step on your path; I'm talking about experiencing the feeling of accomplishment resulting from pursuing your achievement process.

The primary benefit of envisioning the steps of the process from an overview perspective is experiencing the joy and happiness of knowing you are on the path to achieve your goals. Knowing you are on the trail of pursuing your objectives is one of the most rewarding mental states you can put yourself in. It's like looking over the itinerary of the vacation you have planned; there is a certain feeling that comes from the satisfaction of "this is what I am going to do," even though I haven't done it yet or I am only

Chapter 5: Creating a Vision for Your Life

in the process of planning it. I feel it right now in the middle of the night as I am just completing thirty minutes (my perfect time segment) of work on this chapter.

There's no right answer to the number of steps or segments that go into the process of visualizing a goal, but I would suggest you use nine steps in the absence of anything better. Baseball is a beautiful game for many reasons, but one of the reasons some aficionados think it's perfect is that it's divided into nine innings not defined by time, or score, or number of participants' turns. Each inning can take on its own life, depending on what happens in the batter's box. For no reason other than it feels like about the right number, nine is a good divisor to use to break down the path to achieving one of your significant goals.

Contemplate one of your ultimate goals and divide it in a linear fashion into nine "innings," so to speak. Although visualizing the process involves reviewing the (approximately) nine interim steps you will have to go through to achieve your ultimate goal, the exercise of visualizing the process is not the place to focus on the individual steps, only the general timing and order of the steps. Go from the end (the static goal) back to the beginning (the present) and sketch out the broad steps—like chapters or innings—you will undertake to achieve your goal. Again, don't be highly detailed in this exercise; this is the overview of the process, not the detailed determination of the specifics of each step.

CREATE YOUR VISION STATEMENT

Some experts recommend drafting a vision statement to guide you along the way to creating your vision, and you can't say that's a bad idea. It's analogous to a strategic plan for your life or your business. Writing down a vision for accomplishing your goals lends power and commitment to their accomplishment and significantly increases the probability you will achieve them.

Creating the vision process statement is the big itinerary for reaching your goal. Again, it's not a detailed diagram of necessary steps. It's the itinerary, and it helps you understand how things will fit together, the overall timeline of accomplishing your goals, and how you're going to feel as the innings tick by. In the first, second, and third innings, you feel good because you're in the game. You've made the big leagues; you're in control of your destiny, and you're on the path to your success. For each inning, throw out a date for being at that step and jot down a feeling you believe you will be experiencing as you see yourself on the path to achieving your goal. As you envision the process, internalize the feelings about accomplishing each step, particularly the later steps that are closer to achieving the ultimate goal. Similar to the thought process you go through with visualizing the completed static goal, each step can be savored in your conscious and subconscious mind. By visualizing the entire process, you will see your future, the one you are creating for yourself.

Chapter 5: Creating a Vision for Your Life

CHAPTER EXERCISE

Here are some questions and observations to consider when undertaking your visualization exercise. Make it specific and vivid.

1. Visualize the physical details of your future, static vision:
    a. How do you look?
    b. How do you carry yourself?
    c. Where are you?
    d. Where do you live? (Think specifics: what city, state, or country, type of community, house or apartment, style and atmosphere.)
2. What kind of people are in your life?
    a. Are you with another person, a group of people, or are you by yourself?
    b. Who are they?
    c. How do you feel about them?
    d. How do they feel about you?
3. What will you have accomplished already?
    a. How do you feel about your accomplishments?
    b. Are you proud of yourself?
    c. Are those around you proud of you?
4. What does your ideal day look like?
    a. What would you be doing?
    b. How do you see yourself moving forward?
    c. Where do you see yourself going?
    d. What do you believe you're capable of in life?

5. What are the greatest things you could accomplish, given the right circumstances, resources and motivation?
6. What do you wish you could change about the world? What could you contribute to the world that would make you feel proud and content?
7. When you die, what would you want people to say and remember about you?
8. As a final part of this exercise, put yourself in the mind of the future you and offer some advice and guidance to the present you.
9. What will the future you tell the present you that will help the present you achieve the goal?

Action plan for this chapter:
WRITE YOUR PERSONAL VISION STATEMENT.

CHAPTER 6

WHAT IS YOUR LIFE PURPOSE?

The meaning of life is to find your gift.
The purpose of life is to give it away.
—David Viscott

Your life purpose is a deep, philosophical objective that is easy to get preoccupied with. For the purpose of mastering self-discipline, I recommend you not get deeply entwined in different schools of philosophy or you will spend your time trying to figure out a definition of concepts like "life," "purpose" or "meaning." A cynical view of this exercise is if you spend your time pursuing those intellectual questions, you won't have to worry about self-discipline because you won't be doing anything other than philosophizing. So my suggestion is to stay a little more basic when it comes to contemplating your life purpose.

Setting aside deep philosophical inquiry into the meaning of life, your life purpose is a background component to your foundation for mastering self-discipline. There are conflicts in philosophical views about the purpose of one's life, but in its simple form, your life purpose is simply having a reason for living that is greater than yourself. For now, think of your life purpose as the medium- to long-term implementation of your core values and vision with an emphasis on your ethical core values, meaning those that relate to others.

Your life purpose describes doing something meaningful to you that is beyond yourself, something that has significance to other people. Obviously, your life purpose will be in line with your core values and your vision, but its ramifications lie in the effect that you can have on others. What is the importance of your being here and going through the motions of living? Whom do you affect and what significance do your actions and being have on the people around you? What is your contribution to the world? As you can see, these questions can be thought-provoking, and although they are important, if we want to get through the day, we can't obsessively dwell on them. Your greater purpose is evolving day by day as you live your core values and life vision. You are creating your life purpose with every step you take.

The accurate description and/or determination of your life purpose evolves over time. It isn't something you just wake up tomorrow and decide on. Discovering your life purpose is a logical extension of living and implementing your core values and developing and articulating your vision. Your life purpose evolves to be the significance your existence will have on others, and consequently, a measure of the relevance of your life.

If, God forbid, your funeral were three years from today, what would you want people to say about you? He was a great golfer? She was at the top of her club's tennis ladder? Maybe, but wouldn't you rather want people to feel that you had accomplished something important or made a significant contribution to them (or something) with your life? Far be it from me to judge anyone else's life purpose, but I want mine to be a little more significant than being a good golfer or tennis player. (Let me add that I don't

Chapter 6: What Is Your Life Purpose?

have to worry about either of those qualities being included in my epitaph.)

Pull together your core values (beliefs, desires, ideals) along with your vision (where you see yourself at particular times in the reasonably near-term future) and, as you proceed through your personal achievement process, start to decide what your life purpose is and what you want it to be. Let your decision result from the actions of implementing your vision and living what is meaningful to you every day. Your life purpose will evolve from making an impact on family, a business, your community, or some contribution that you make to the greater good.

Finding your life purpose is a long-term journey. A person's life purpose is an evolving thing that is discovered over time by living in pursuit of her core values and vision. You should have confidence that you will discover it, but you should also realize that you are living it through your daily actions that are bearing out your core values. So relax about it, but keep striving for it at the same time. Your core values are things you can think about and decide on, and your vision is a trajectory and a goal you can map out. Your life purpose is more indirect. It becomes the evolutionary result of living your core values.

Don't be concerned that your life purpose has to be something world-changing, because that probably isn't in the cards for most of us. It may be contributing to a good relationship or being a valued parent, or an extraordinary friend. Your purpose might be being a positive force in your professional firm, charitable organization or community. Think about the influence that each of us can have on others by being kind or helpful; many times we aren't even told of the positive effect we have had on someone, but that person carries with them the benefit of their interaction with us. These are the consequences resulting from your core values that combine to create a meaningful life purpose. Your greater meaning in life might be having done something unadvertised that is significant and meaningful to someone else.

So don't be preoccupied with trying to determine your exact life purpose; realize that it is developing as you proceed through your life vision. It is certainly beneficial to contemplate the importance of the commitment you have to yourself and the world around you, and those thoughts may inform your decisions about your core values. But think about it from a larger perspective: even great historical figures weren't focused on their legacies, they were focused on accomplishing the important tasks in front of them. If you keep your focus on the goals that you identify as significant to you and your mission in life, your life purpose will take care of itself.

CHAPTER 7

DEVELOPING YOUR GUIDING PRINCIPLES

Whether you think you can or whether you think you can't, you're right.
—Henry Ford

Your guiding principles help give structure to your daily life. They should be tailored to help you feel good about yourself and give you the confidence, control and structure to be successful in your daily endeavors. If you're only alive for this minute (and that is an absolute fact), how do you want to live it? Do you want to live it standing tall, feeling good and moving forward with your life? Or, do you want to live it slouched in your chair, arteries constricted and muscles atrophying? The answer seems pretty clear to me.

The goal of this chapter is to alert you to the importance of guiding principles and help you develop a set of principles that work for you every hour of every day. Guiding principles are a little bit like the Ten Commandments, but they don't have to be moralistic or imposed by a higher being. They are created by you and should be designed to meet your specific needs and support your objectives, and they should address your personal strengths and weaknesses. Of course, they can have a moral/ethical foundation if that conforms to your values, but they can be completely agnostic as well.

As a concept, your guiding principles should do the following:

1. They should make you feel good about yourself and encourage you to know you are moving forward with the vision for your life.

2. They should be tailored to support you in overcoming any weaknesses you have in your daily conduct.

3. They should be designed to encourage you to reach for achievement in your life.

4. And overall, they should help you structure your daily activities in order to achieve your goals.

Guiding principles are daily standards that you rely on in moments of uncertainty to provide direction for the next hour of your life. Every minute and every hour of your life is a choice, and each choice that you make is life-enhancing or life-diminishing.[8] To ensure that your choices are positive and life-enhancing, you must develop tenets of conduct that work for you. They are critically important to keep you motivated and on track in your quest for the self-discipline necessary to achieve your goals.

I have developed a set of guiding principles that work for me that I will share with you as an example. My guiding principles have been developed (and changed) to meet my personal strengths and weaknesses, and yours should focus on you, not me. When you develop yours and you try to live by them, it is important *not* to set an impossible standard of excellence in attaining them.

---
[8] Deborah Szekely, cofounder of Rancho La Puerta fitness resort in Tecate, BC, Mexico.

Chapter 7: Developing Your Guiding Principles

I suggest that your principles be current and active and, if you have a reason, you can break these rules from time to time (and be prepared that you will). You have to struggle to find a way of living that works for you, and you'll have to practice applying the principles that help you succeed with each day of your life.

As part of the process of mastering self-discipline, I recommend that you honestly evaluate your strengths and weaknesses. Your guiding principles must be designed to help you focus on your strengths and overcome your weaknesses. They are the spiritual "fallback" that you will rely on for guidance in your daily life.

I am going to give you my guiding principles as a starting place, but I caution you that these are designed to accentuate my strengths (in my opinion) and support my weaknesses (in my opinion) and they won't necessarily be right for you. But they work pretty well for me. I will briefly discuss my reasoning for each one—again, to support your thinking process as you develop your own. I will also propose a number of them at the end of the chapter for your consideration. Here are my guiding principles:

1. I am *this* man.
2. This moment is my life.
3. I am action this moment, not thought.
4. I use this moment to move ahead of the curve.
5. My Being controls my body.
6. I strive this hour to focus on the values that advance me.
7. I pause this moment to organize my direction.
8. I delegate all tasks to my team members.
9. I will greet this day as if it is my last.
10. Guide me, God.

Following is the underlying rationale behind each of my guiding principles.

I AM *THIS* MAN.

This principle establishes immediate self-confidence. It reminds me where I am in my life and it credits me for all the good things I have done. It recognizes the challenging road I have successfully traveled so far. The principle does not dwell on anything negative about my past or any failings that I might have, and it acts as a basis for me to confidently move forward.

In 1988, George H. W. Bush had been Ronald Reagan's vice president for eight years. Although Mr. Bush had been a Navy fighter pilot who was shot down in the Pacific in World War II, a successful entrepreneur, a congressman, director of the Central Intelligence Agency, Ambassador to the United Nations and vice president, he was perceived somewhat as a "second fiddle" to President Reagan, who was known as the "Great Communicator." Bush was labeled a wimp by many in the press, and in the early days of the presidential campaign, he had yet to obtain the confidence of the public. There was a time in his campaign when he was seventeen points behind his opponent but, as the presidential campaign rolled along, the tide began to change from Governor Michael Dukakis to Vice President Bush. I remember listening to his speech at the national convention where he was nominated to succeed Reagan, and as he recited a long list of impressive contributions to the well-being of the United States, his refrain after each item was, "*I am that man.*" He said it with a cadence and repetition that was powerful and almost musical. Those words have stayed with me ever since I first heard them and, as we all know, George H. W. Bush was elected the 41st president of the United States.

Chapter 7: Developing Your Guiding Principles

As I developed my personal guiding principles over the years, I wanted to start with one that would set a positive feeling for me as I addressed the issues in front of me for the day. I need to begin my guiding principles by feeling good about myself and having the confidence that I can overcome any challenges that I may face in the next hours of my life. By way of contrast, the first guiding principle in Og Mandino's brilliant short book, *The Greatest Salesman in the World*, is "Today I begin a new life."[9] For many years, I used this as my first guiding principle, but I eventually decided that it was not positive enough for me. It reminded me of being at the bottom of a big mountain, and the notion that I had all this challenge in front of me with no credit for everything I had already accomplished was not encouraging enough for me. So over time, I evolved my first guiding principle to be "I am *this* man."

THIS MOMENT IS MY LIFE.

This principle brings me to the here and now, and it takes me away from the fantasy of yesterday or the future. The present is the only life that we have, and many of us spend far too much mental time in the past and in the future. Spending time in the past or the future takes away from the importance of the present and the reality that the present is the only time segment that we can do anything with. There's nothing wrong with thinking about the future as long as that fantasy is used for planning purposes, and not for worrying. But it should not be used as a crutch for the false belief that some emotional satisfaction will be achieved in the future. In

---

[9] The Scroll Marked I, *The Greatest Salesman in the World* (Bantam Books, 1968) by Og Mandino. Mandino died in 1996, having written more than twenty-five books that sold over fifty million copies.

reality, the only emotional satisfaction that is achievable in life is the emotional satisfaction of the present. And your emotional satisfaction with your life is a conscious, present choice.

Over the years, I have often caught myself being bored with the moment and wanting to get to the next hour or day of my life. Michael Pollan, author of the 2006 food industry exposé *The Omnivore's Dilemma*, talks about living in the moment by saying, "If I'm chopping onions, just chop onions." One of the ways he realized the joy of the moment was through his love of cooking and learning that if you're chopping onions, just chop onions. Live in the present. A second pitfall that is easy to drop into is the momentary negative thinking of some argument you're having or some other negative thought process that drains your positive mental energy and diverts your attention from positively moving forward. There is virtually no value in succumbing to that mental negativism, and it doubly affects you because it subtracts from your advancement. In absolute fact, "this moment *is* my life," and I am foolish if I don't appreciate that fact, enjoy this moment, and productively employ the moment to advance myself toward achieving my goals.

I AM ACTION THIS MOMENT, NOT THOUGHT.

This principle focuses on the importance of accomplishing some task rather than imagining (either positive or negative) something unreal. Action is real and thought is fantasy. Of course, there is nothing wrong with thinking, planning, and envisioning the future, but this principle reminds me to get something done *right now*. Generally speaking, it is the failure to act that causes stagnation and frustration, not the failure to think about acting. The principle is stated in the present tense, as all guiding principles should be, and it brings the listener to the precipice of this instant. What are you going to do now? This principle tells me to do something, right now.

Assuming that I have a set of core values, a vision, and a life purpose that are in alignment, any action I undertake should positively move me forward in my life. Implementing some action—any action—in pursuit of my goals is the very definition of happiness. One of the tactics of self-discipline is to have a list of tasks you are in the process of doing to implement your goals, and this guiding principle takes you to your list to accomplish something right now.

I USE THIS MOMENT TO MOVE AHEAD OF THE CURVE.

I use two visual examples to illustrate this principle. Imagine two surfers who are catching a wave on a beautiful sunny morning. One of them is paddling furiously, right behind the crest of the wave. The wave rolls along and he is desperately trying to keep up with it, expending a huge amount of energy trying to reach the crest. He is paddling and paddling ... paddling himself to near exhaustion. The second surfer is about ten yards to the right of the first surfer. When the wave approached them, he propelled himself just a little bit harder than the first surfer and he reached the crest of the wave and got a few feet ahead of it. He is effortlessly riding the wave, skimming through the water just ahead of the peak of the wave and using gravity and his skill of balance to navigate his comfortable ride.

The difference between these two surfers is remarkable. The one who used a little more effort (and intelligence) at the outset of the activity is far better off than the one who never got ahead of the wave. The amount of energy each one expended catching the wave is insignificantly different. However, one ride will be joyful and effortless while the other will be a constant struggle.

Another vivid example of this principle is the snowplow that's going just a little bit too slow and struggling to push a big mound of snow in front of its blade. You can see it struggling and hear the roar of its mighty diesel engine, reminding you of the delightful 1930 tale, *The Little Engine That Could*. Visualize the straining snowplow as compared to a second one that is blasting through the snow, a few miles an hour faster than the first one, and the snow is shooting high above the snowplow truck, almost making it appear to be a snowblower instead of a snowplow. The driver of the second plow has figured out how to expend just a little more energy in the execution of the job, and the benefits reaped from the extra energy are substantial.

There seems to be a "curve" in almost every activity in our lives, and there is a smart technique that can be employed to get ahead of that curve and be in control of the exercise as opposed to being a little behind the momentum of the activity. To my way of thinking, it's a difference of about 10 percent of energy: you can either be 5 percent behind the crest of the activity or 5 percent ahead of it, and the difference between those two places is immense. I try to be aware of this reality and "get after" the task, so to speak. I always try to make sure I am ahead of the curve.

MY BEING CONTROLS MY BODY.

I don't know if there's a higher power in the universe, but I am sure there is a higher authority over my physical actions than just my muscles. We all have a higher spirit within ourselves that we call upon to guide us in our everyday lives. This guiding principle acknowledges that fact and calls upon our "Being" (our soul, our spirit, our God, whatever works for you) to guide our mortal selves in our daily lives.

"My Being controls my body" acknowledges the higher spirit—my conscience—that guides me through my life. Our higher spirit sets our priorities and core values, and our spirit is clearly superior to our bodies. I like to think of my body as the worker bee and my "Being" as the chief executive officer. In my life, my Being sets my goals and priorities, and my body does what it's told to do. This principle acknowledges the subservient position that my body occupies in relation to my Being and it makes necessary tasks easier to accomplish. It's easier for my Being to order something done, and I know my body just exists to follow orders.

One of the experts I interviewed for this book, Jamie Metzl, suggested that he never tolerates negotiating with himself to accomplish tasks. In the struggle between his Being and his body, he never allows his body to win the struggle. In fact, he won't even allow there to be an internal argument, assuring that his Being always controls the action.[10]

I STRIVE THIS HOUR TO FOCUS ON THE VALUES THAT ADVANCE ME.

Until a few years ago, for me, this principle was "I strive this hour to control the forces that work against me." After thinking about the negative tone of the older principle, I evolved it to the present one that simply reinforces my positive values and how they support me in my flow of daily activities. My core values

---

10 Perhaps that's why Jamie has run fifteen marathons, authored six highly acclaimed books, and obtained both a PhD and a law degree.

support my positive existence, and I want to constantly reinforce them. I want to constantly remind myself that my values stand behind everything I do and they exist to positively advance me on my quest to achieve my goals.

By constantly focusing on my core values, I continually remind myself of my fundamental beliefs as the basis for my actions. Earlier, I defined happiness as doing things in pursuit of my core values, so reverting back to my core values reinforces that happiness and encourages me to move forward on the productive path of effectuating them.

I PAUSE THIS MOMENT TO ORGANIZE MY DIRECTION.

Stop, take stock of where I am right now, and organize my immediate path forward. The benefit of this principle is self-evident. It requires me to get out of my head, my possible worrying about the future or obsessing about the past, and focus on the moment and what I am going to do with the next hour of my life. That is the only real control we have over ourselves—the next hour or so of our lives. So stop a moment, reflect on where you are in the process, and organize yourself to move forward positively.

I DELEGATE ALL TASKS TO MY TEAM MEMBERS.

It is important to be aware of what jobs or tasks I am good at doing and what types of things I'm not. It is unproductive to try to force myself to do things that don't fit my personality if I can possibly delegate those tasks to others around me. One of the keys to leadership is understanding the personalities of those around us and helping them find tasks that fit their dispositions. People want to do things that make them feel fulfilled, and I don't want to spend time doing things that don't really work for me, so I go out of my way to try to delegate tasks to those around me. Of course, if you are at the stage of your development where you have to do most everything yourself, you simply have to force yourself to accomplish a variety of tasks, even if they don't suit your personal preferences. Soon enough, you will be at the stage where you have other folks around you to delegate less desirable tasks to.

I WILL GREET THIS DAY AS IF IT IS MY LAST.

First of all, I accept the reality that it might be my last one. We certainly never know, right? If today was really my last day, what do I want to do with it? Do I want to be worrying or getting down on myself for something I am not particularly proud of? Or, do I want to be happy, satisfied with myself, and moving forward with things that are important to my life vision? There is no doubt where I come out on these questions. I will greet (and live) this day as if it is my last.

GUIDE ME, GOD.

I am not particularly religious, and I would be the first to admit my uncertainty about the existence of a higher being. However, I do want to believe there is something, some force, some "being," possibly, that is greater than we individually are. I also realize that many people—probably most—are believers in some God, some higher power. Perhaps this principle simply grounds me in the acknowledgment that I may not be the final arbiter of my life. I include this last principle as one of my guideposts to daily living, and I think it is a worthwhile one.

These are the guiding principles I fall back on five or ten times a day. Whenever I am floundering—and believe me, it happens a lot—I rely on these refreshers of what's important to get restarted. Sometimes I will focus on one or two of them more than the rest, but they are all important to me. Maybe guiding principles are like prayers to a religious person. By that comparison, I certainly understand the benefit of prayer, because stepping back for a minute and reflecting on what guides you through life is definitely worthwhile.

EXAMPLES OF GUIDING PRINCIPLES THAT YOU MIGHT CONSIDER FOR YOURSELF:

I will start with three sets of guiding principles from presidents of the United States.

Thomas Jefferson, the third president of the United States, made a list of his guiding principles. These principles were fundamental in how President Jefferson lived his life.[11]

---

11 I have taken this information from https://www.wow4u.com/guidingprinciples/.

Chapter 7: Developing Your Guiding Principles

1. Never put off till tomorrow what you can do today.
2. Never trouble another for what you can do yourself.
3. Never spend your money before you have it.
4. Never buy what you do not want, because it is cheap; it will be dear to you.
5. Pride costs us more than hunger, thirst, and cold.
6. We never repent of having eaten too little.
7. Nothing is troublesome that we do willingly.
8. How much pain have cost us the evils which have never happened.
9. Take things always by their smooth handle.
10. When angry, count ten before you speak; if very angry, a hundred.

According to the same source, another president of the United States, Abraham Lincoln, said the following related to following guiding principles: "Do not worry; eat three square meals a day; say your prayers; be courteous to your creditors; keep your digestion good; exercise; go slow and easy. Maybe there are other things your special case requires to make you happy, but my friend, these I reckon will give you a good lift."

And finally, President Dwight Eisenhower is quoted as saying, "Do some self-reflection and try to contemplate your innermost motivations in life."

Years ago I had the good fortune to discover *The Greatest Salesman in the World* by Og Mandino.[12] It is a beautiful short allegory that is definitely worth reading. Worked into the ancient story are the following principles described by Mandino as "Ten Scrolls":

1. Today I begin a new life.
2. I will greet this day with love in my heart.

---
12 Og Mandino, *The Greatest Salesman in the World* (Bantam Books, 1968).

3. I will persist until I succeed.
4. I am nature's greatest miracle.
5. I will live this day as if it is my last.
6. Today I will be master of my emotions.
7. I will laugh at the world.
8. Today I will multiply my value a hundredfold.
9. I will act now.
10. I will pray for guidance.

The final set of guiding principles that I will include here is the Prayer of St. Francis. I have committed it to memory and I rely on it frequently.

> Lord, make me an instrument of thy peace,
> Where there is hatred, let me sow love;
> where there is injury, pardon;
> where there is doubt, faith;
> where there is despair, hope;
> where there is darkness, light;
> where there is sadness, joy;
> O Divine Master, grant that I may not so much seek to be consoled as to console;
> to be understood as to understand;
> to be loved as to love.
> For it is in giving that we receive;
> it is in pardoning that we are pardoned;
> and it is in dying that we are born to eternal life.

Chapter 7: Developing Your Guiding Principles

CHAPTER EXERCISE

1. Recognize the importance of having guiding principles in your life.
2. Use the suggested guiding principles in this chapter as a starting place and develop (about) ten principles to rely on as a standard in your day-to-day living.
3. Commit them to memory.
4. Acknowledge that your guiding principles will continue to evolve as you develop your strengths and overcome your weaknesses.

CHAPTER 8

THE IMPORTANCE OF ALIGNMENT

Alignment is the connectivity between your soul and your daily activities. There is an obvious relationship between your Being and your body, your soul and your actions. Your daily activities are the manifestation of your greater self—good or bad—and the more your actions are lined up and in synch with your core values and your vision, the more efficient and happy you will be in actualizing your life purpose. The definition of the word "alignment" is the "correct positioning of different components with respect to each other so they perform properly."[13] As it relates to the connection between your soul and your actions, alignment is the synchronization of all the components of the personal and professional achievement process.

In this chapter, I am going to fast-forward and talk generally about goals and tasks, although the detailed discussions of those subjects are deferred to Chapter 10 (goals) and Chapter 11 (tasks). Your goals follow your core values (beliefs), your vision (your static objective at the end of the rainbow), and your life purpose (the significance of your existence beyond yourself). Goals are the objectives you strive for in order to effectuate your core values. Tasks are the necessary actions that have to be com-

---

13 Encarta Dictionary: English (North America).

pleted to achieve your goals, and it's the tasks that require self-discipline. The reality is that many tasks aren't particularly enjoyable, but they can certainly be made more enjoyable, and doing them can even make you happy if you are pursuing your core values and the vision for your life.

If your goals don't logically follow your core values, your personal achievement process is in disharmony and there is no logical progression between the steps required to implement your vision. If you're not in alignment, you are constantly trying to force yourself to do things that aren't in pursuit of what is truly important to you. A synchronous state of alignment enables you to be engaged in your activities, happily pursuing truly important goals, and easily overcoming any unpleasantness involved in doing the necessary tasks on your list of to-dos. Ironically, being in alignment puts you in a much greater state of happiness as you execute the daily tasks and activities to achieve your goals. By definition, happiness is doing the actions and undertakings in pursuit of your core values.

By contrast, if you are having difficulty moving forward or you find yourself just plain stuck, you should probably take a look at the path you are on and ask yourself if you are in a personal achievement process of actualizing core values and vision you feel good about. You might find you are working for someone else's core values or not being true to yourself. An example of this situation might be a college student who is pursuing a degree in something his parents want him to pursue or a son or daughter working in a family business that isn't really what they want to do. If you find yourself in this predicament, reevaluate your core values and look at the goals you have set for yourself to make sure they are aligned in a way suited to your true vision for yourself.

Chapter 8: The Importance of Alignment

The best way to understand and appreciate the benefits of alignment is to think of sometime in the past when you were very engaged in a specific activity. An example might be a challenging work project or an academic endeavor. Back up to that time and think about the entire spectrum of feelings, and the particular feeling you had toward the particular activity. Although different words could be used to describe those feelings, let's define the range of the feelings applicable to all activities at one end of the continuum as drudgery (boredom, annoyance), moving up the spectrum to neutral, then to engagement (interested, happy), then to flow (enamored, ecstatic).

To envision the spectrum, at the undesirable end, there is the drudgery of doing some task you absolutely don't like to do. Examples could be things like doing some boring, seemingly unnecessary task at work, cleaning out the trash cans, cleaning the bathroom, doing laundry, the kinds of tasks we try to delegate as soon as we can afford to hire someone to do them for us. Or unfortunately, this end of the spectrum might include some things we should be doing, like exercise, eating healthfully or studying. Moving up on the spectrum, there is the neutral feeling of doing something you simply have to do (or maybe even want to do), but you don't have particular feelings about it. Examples could be things like showering/shaving/putting on makeup, walking the dog, fixing dinner, driving to work—the kinds of things some people like to do, other people don't, some don't even think about, but which are not particularly remarkable. Then there are the tasks we actually get engaged in. Engagement means you are "into" the task, enjoying it, focusing on it and relishing the accomplishment of the activity. For me, an example would be doing a crossword puzzle or working on some home improvement project like building a cabinet. For a college student, it might be the feeling he gets when writing a paper, after the original procrastination and resistance to the project is past, and when the satisfaction of really putting it together finally begins. Being engaged is an enjoyable state to be in, one providing personal satisfaction from accomplishing the tasks at hand. And, if you think about it, the reason engagement is so satisfying is that you are positively moving forward on some enjoyable activity or worthwhile vision you have for yourself. You are checking necessary tasks off your list and achieving some goal—big or small—that is important to you. That feels really good, and we would like to experience the feeling with almost everything we do, especially the things we have to do.

Moving up the continuum of feelings, beyond the state of engagement is the state of flow, which one author has described as "engagement on steroids."[14] It is the feeling of being completely absorbed in an activity to the extent that time escapes us and our being is totally engrossed in the joy and the focus of the task. So, how do we possibly get to the peak of the spectrum, the state of flow? Daniel Pink talks about the three elements of intrinsic motivation—autonomy, mastery and purpose—in his excellent book, *Drive: The Surprising Truth About What Motivates Us*.[15] Getting to flow is not an everyday occurrence and, while you should always hope to achieve it, you shouldn't be disappointed if most of the time you are only striving for it. What matters is that you know what it is and that it's sometimes attainable.

To whet your appetite for the enviable state of flow, the brilliant psychologist and author Mihaly Csikszentmihalyi describes

---
14 Bill Burnett and Dale Evans, *Designing Your Life: How to Build a Well-Lived, Joyful Life* (New York: Knopf, 2016), 44.
15 Daniel H. Pink, *Drive: The Surprising Truth About What Motivates Us* (New York: Riverhead Books, 2009).

Chapter 8: The Importance of Alignment

how it feels to be in flow and suggests you can only get to the state of flow when you are both highly challenged and comfortably functioning at a high skill level.[16] He characterizes the state as:

1. Completely involved in what we are doing—focused, concentrated;
2. A great sense of ecstasy—of being outside everyday reality;
3. Great inner clarity—knowing what needs to be done and how well we are doing;
4. Knowing the activity is doable—that our skills are adequate to the task;
5. A sense of serenity—no worries about oneself, and a feeling of growing beyond the boundaries of the ego;
6. Timelessness—thoroughly focused on the present, hours seem to pass by in minutes;
7. Intrinsic motivation—whatever produces flow becomes its own reward.

Isn't this where we want to try to be all the time? Wouldn't it be wonderful if every hour of our working day could feel like a great musician must feel when she is performing something she loves to do in front of a packed concert hall of loving patrons? Yes, I know this is an ideal fantasy, but we can't possibly get there if we don't understand it and also believe it is attainable.

The entire personal achievement process which incorporates mastering self-discipline involves finding your soul (Chapter 3), defining your core values (Chapter 4), and creating your vision (your plan and your destination—Chapter 5). When you achieve the synchrony of those foundational steps, you can then establish your goals, identify the tasks necessary to achieve the goals, and enforce the self-discipline to execute the necessary tasks to achieve

---

16 Mihaly Csikszentmihalyi, "Flow," TED Talk, February 2004, https://www.youtube.com/watch?v=I_u-Eh3h-7Mo. Csikszentmihalyi originated the concept of flow in the mid-1970s.

those goals. Believe it or not, you will enjoy the ride and enjoy the success of your accomplishments. The successful implementation of this continuum will lead you to a life purpose that is worthwhile and is executed in conformance with your well-thought-out ideals. Having all these steps in alignment—in synchronization—is the key to getting our necessary tasks to at least the engagement level and, hopefully, the flow level at least some of the time. I know the successful execution of this process is easier said than done, but in the final analysis, I have just described a personal achievement process that includes the mastery of self-discipline. If you pursue an aligned personal achievement process, your tasks will be easier and your daily happiness will be greater because you will be on a continuum conformed to your fundamental beliefs and desires for yourself.

SECTION III
PLAN OF ACTION FOR SELF-DISCIPLINE

CHAPTER 9

INTEGRITY OF COMMITMENT

The quality of a person's life is in direct proportion to their commitment to excellence, regardless of their chosen field of endeavor.
—Vince Lombardi

We have established the fact that exercising self-discipline is not effortless, but it certainly can be made easier than the simple application of brute force to make you do things you don't want to do. If your only motivational tactic is to suck it up and get the job done, you might be successful at accomplishing a few tasks, but the technique won't sustain you. You need a broader strategy to develop the habit of self-discipline to execute the necessary tasks to accomplish your goals. In my research, I have uncovered one character trait above all others that is fundamental to the mastery of self-discipline: integrity of commitment.

A commitment is a promise or firm decision to do something, made to yourself or to another. Commitments are usually made because something needs to be done but there is no assurance it will be done, so someone formally agrees to do it. In the law, an enforceable commitment is a legal contract that obligates the promising party and entitles the promised party to remedies if the commitment is broken. The remedies for breach of the commitment range from monetary damages to specific performance, requiring the breaching party to do the act that was promised. Regardless of the remedy, the law will enforce a promise between two parties if they each have the capacity to enter into the contract.

In *The Seven Habits of Highly Effective People*, Stephen Covey defines integrity as the characteristic of keeping commitments to yourself and others.[17] Covey maintains that integrity includes but goes beyond honesty. Honesty is telling the truth, conforming our words to reality. Integrity is conforming reality to our words—in other words, keeping promises and fulfilling expectations.

Interestingly, it seems our willingness to keep commitments to others is often easier than our willingness to keep commitments to ourselves. Most people wouldn't think of breaking a promise to a friend to do something for her, but when it comes to blowing off a pledge to ourselves, we can come up with any excuse, or even no excuse at all. Why the distinction? Why are we willing to let ourselves down when we wouldn't think of letting our neighbor down? We seem to value a promise to another as more important than a pledge to ourselves. You would think each of us is the most important person in the world to ourselves and we wouldn't break our own promises, but that seems not to be the case.

There's an interesting element in contract law that may explain this dichotomy. To be enforceable, a legal contract requires consideration, defined as something of value given by one party in return for the promise of the other party to the contract. When you make a commitment to another person, you have entered into an agreement having some semblance of consideration, if not actual consideration. You said, "I will come over and help you clean your

---

[17] Stephen R. Covey, *The Seven Habits of Highly Effective People* (New York: Simon & Schuster, 1989), 195.

Chapter 9: Integrity of Commitment

garage," whether or not your friend said, "I will pay you $25." At the very least, your friend has the expectation that you will perform your commitment. The fact that two parties are involved in the commitment sets an expectation, at least, if not full consideration to the bargain in many cases. You have gotten something in return for your commitment to perform X, and something in return makes you feel more obligated to follow through on your commitment. But when you say to yourself, "I'm going to the gym in the morning," there is no consideration given in return for making the commitment. Or, at best, the consideration is that you are going to gain the benefits of health and fitness; but to be hyper-legal about it, future consideration is no consideration at all. So, your personal commitment to go to the gym (or to do X) is a one-sided promise that needs a little boost to be enforceable.

There are several techniques to try to build some contract-type consideration into our personal commitments. The first is to make your personal commitments into bargains in which you give yourself little rewards for keeping the commitment. "After I go to the gym in the morning, I'm going to take a 20-minute Jacuzzi." Or, "After I study for three hours, I am going out with my friends." Turn these commitments into bargains where there is some form of consideration promised to yourself in exchange for accomplishing the task you committed to do. A second method is accountability to another person for the commitments you make. Involving another person in your commitment process is definitely beneficial, probably for the same reasons that we are inclined to keep commitments to other people. If another person is involved in the deal, all of the emotions relating to disappointment and regret are brought up, and that accountability to another person helps motivate us to do the things that we need to do.

In the final analysis, the habit and practice of commitment is at the core of self-discipline because the essence of self-discipline is the internal strength to honor the commitments you make to yourself. Keeping your personal promises is one of the hardest parts of life and one of the most basic components of the quality of one's character. It is important we make these personal commitments, make them reasonable and achievable, have the grit to follow through with necessary action, have a simple measuring stick to track them, reward ourselves for accomplishing them, and don't punish ourselves for not achieving perfection. If you develop the ability to enforce commitments to yourself, then you can make them for every worthwhile goal in your life, and if you have the habit of meeting them, you can accomplish anything. We all have to climb the mountain one step at a time. And, your time starts now.

CHAPTER EXERCISE

1. Practice making small commitments to yourself.
2. Keep them.
3. This is a habit that can be learned.

CHAPTER 10

UNDERSTANDING AND ESTABLISHING GOALS

If you don't know where you're going, you'll end up someplace else.
—*Yogi Berra*

On October 4, 1957, the Soviet Union launched a 23-inch polished metal sphere called Sputnik into a low space orbit for the first time in human history. The spacecraft orbited Earth for three weeks before its batteries died, then silently for two more months before falling back into the atmosphere. The satellite traveled about 18,000 miles an hour, taking 96.2 minutes to complete each of its orbits. Sputnik burned up on January 4, 1958, while reentering Earth's atmosphere after three months, 1,440 completed orbits of Earth, and a distance traveled of about 43 million miles.[18]

Americans were shocked and somewhat frightened by the Russian accomplishment. The Russians' apparent space conquest solidified the belief that our scientific and technical progress was second-rate at a time when the Cold War was on everyone's mind. There were fears that Russia's domination of space would be used militarily to dominate the West.

---

18 "Sputnik and the Dawn of the Space Age," NASA History website, last updated October 10, 2007, https://history.nasa.gov/sputnik/, and Wikipedia, "Sputnik 1," last updated October 16, 2019, https://en.wikipedia.org/wiki/Sputnik_1.

In response to Russia's accomplishment, Congress passed the National Aeronautics and Space Act of 1958 creating the National Aeronautics and Space Administration, the agency known as NASA. Over the next few years, it seemed that the United States still continued to flounder, continuously following the Russians in second place. Soviet cosmonaut Yuri Gagarin orbited the Earth on April 12, 1961. The US followed closely, successfully launching Alan Shepard into space on May 5, 1961, although he only flew a short, suborbital flight instead of orbiting the globe like Gagarin did. We were in the game, but we certainly were not leading the charge.

A few weeks after Alan Shepard's flight, President John F. Kennedy was scheduled to speak at Rice University in Houston, the home of NASA, the fledgling organization then employing about 8,000 scientists and engineers dedicated to "provide for research into the problems of flight within and outside the earth's atmosphere."[19] In the sweltering heat of that summer day in Texas and in response to Russia's apparent dominance in early space exploration, President Kennedy established the nearly unimaginable goal of the United States sending a man to the moon within a mere ten years. What was incredible about creating this unfathomable dream was that here was a man—a leader—setting a goal without the complete organization, the technology or the capability to achieve it; he just laid out the hope, promise and bold intention that it could be done! And eight years and two months later, Apollo 11 was launched by a Saturn V rocket from the Kennedy Space Center, hurling three American astronauts 240,000 miles toward the lunar surface. On July 21, 1969, Neil Armstrong stepped onto the Sea of Tranquility and uttered the famous words "One small step for

---

19 https://history.nasa.gov.

Chapter 10: Understanding and Establishing Goals

man, one giant leap for mankind" as he exited the lunar module Eagle about six hours after landing on the moon, effectively ending the space race and fulfilling the national goal proposed by President Kennedy in 1961.

A goal is a specific milestone of accomplishment aligned with realizing your core values and the vision for your life. Susan Ward, the well-known and respected business author, defines goal setting as "the process of deciding what you want to accomplish and devising a plan to achieve the result you desire."[20] There is great power in having clearly defined, purposeful goals and, even more importantly, having the character, commitment and willpower to act on them.

Goals tend to be long on direction and short on specific tactics. This subtle difference highlights the difference between goals and tasks, which are discussed in Chapter 13. Goals are like the architect's drawings and tasks are the orders of the day for the on-site contractor. Neither goals nor tasks can complete the job independent of one another; the objectives and the detailed steps work hand in glove to succeed.

There are many interesting observations about goals and goal setting. First, almost all successful people regularly establish goals and commit to them. There is a certain reality to that fact, and it tells us not to "fight city hall"—just get with the program and recognize that goal setting works, at least for those successful winners. So, why not believe in it? Better yet, why not commit to it? Second, I can't promise you will achieve all your goals, but I can promise you won't get any farther than your goals. That's another reality of the life-planning technique

---

20 Susan Ward, "Goal Setting Practice for Business Success," The Balance:Small Business, updated November 16, 2018, https://www.thebalancesmb.com/goal-setting-2948135.

of goal setting. It sets a subconscious standard for you and it helps create a focus and a vision of how to accomplish the goals. Without clear goals, you are a rudderless ship foundering in the ocean. The author and great motivational speaker Zig Ziglar is quoted as saying, "A goal properly set is halfway reached." And finally, I have come to the conclusion that there's no cheating your way to achieving your goals—it's the small choices you make every hour of every day that get you to your goals. Goal setting works; you can and should take advantage of its benefits, and you can and will achieve what you clearly identify as your objectives in life if you follow the principles of establishing clear goals. The more passionately you commit to them, the more certain you are to achieve them.

The internet is replete with authors, web pages, and advice about goals and goal setting. When synthesizing the knowledge of the experts in this area, one of the first things you come upon is the acronym SMART. Goals must be SMART:

1. Specific
2. Measurable (or some say Motivational)
3. Achievable or Attainable
4. Realistic (or maybe Relevant?)
5. Time-sensitive

According to smart-goals-guide.com, the acronym SMART first appeared in a November 1981 *Management Review* article entitled "There's a S.M.A.R.T. Way to Write Management Goals and Objectives," written by George Doran, Arthur Miller, and James Cunningham. The acronym was picked up around the world by companies and consultants, and it has proved extremely valuable. Over the years, variants of the acronym have evolved, but the one I suggest here is the most common.

Chapter 10: Understanding and Establishing Goals

SPECIFIC

One of the benefits of having a defined goal is creating a subconscious benchmark—an objective—to achieve, and the more specificity you embed in the visualization, the more likely it is the goal will serve its purpose for you. A vague goal is nothing more than an idle dream, an unachievable fantasy. If your stated goal is not specific enough, it is difficult to define success in achieving it. Here is a short comparison of non-specific goals to specific, affirmative goals to consider as examples:

Non-Specific / Too Generalized	Specific and Affirmative
1. Get out of debt	1. Pay off $3,200 of credit card debt within 24 months
2. Lose weight	2. Weigh 115 pounds by March 31
3. Own my own business	3. Write a business plan for my consulting practice
4. Be a professional speaker	4. Outline two speeches and contact a local speaking bureau

It is psychologically helpful to state your specific goals in the affirmative rather than the negative. Most experts suggest you should only have three to five current goals you are working on. Any more than that will cause you to be scattered in your efforts to achieve them. It's simply not possible to focus the required amount of energy on too many diverse goals, and that is certainly true if the goals are in the same general areas of your life. For instance, trying to get your master's degree in chemistry is a worthwhile goal, but don't complicate it by trying to learn a new foreign language at the same time. In fact, I strongly suggest you try to have only one significant goal in each area of your life. You might concurrently have a professional/academic goal (change jobs, complete an academic program, start a business), a social goal (relationship or other social commitment), a personal goal (health and fitness, pursuit of some worthwhile purpose), and possibly one more goal in another area of your life. Without overloading yourself with too many goals, however, there is definitely a benefit to having a diversity of goals: that enables you to productively change focus regularly and contribute your efforts to an unrelated goal.

Your goals should be defined with clarity and purpose, and there is no better way to approach this end than by concisely writing goals in a journal or planner that you regularly revisit. One recognized expert, Brian Tracy, suggests rewriting goals every day for thirty days without even referring to the previous day's statement of them. Writing down your goals enables you to make them feel more real, as opposed to idle fantasies, and you will begin to prioritize your actions and develop the belief that you will achieve the goals. By writing your desires and goals on a piece of paper, you send a message that these thoughts are more important than the scores of thousands of other thoughts you have in a given day, and your mind starts to filter out the unimportant things and focuses only on the important tasks ahead of you.

Tony Robbins, the great visionary of self-motivation philosophy, suggests you should visualize your goals as though you have already achieved them. That mindfulness practice will help to establish the subconscious road map to take you to the place of reaching your outcome goals. In *The Monk Who Sold His Ferrari*, a beautiful allegory about a burned-out lawyer who became a monk, the protagonist says mapping out goals releases the creative juices that get you on your path of purpose.[21] On a psy-

---

21 Robin Sharma, *The Monk Who Sold His Ferrari* (HarperSanFrancisco, 1999), 81.

chological level, if you are committed to your well-aligned goals, you will seek the responsibility of performing the tasks to achieve those goals.

EXERCISE

1. Identify three to five goals for yourself.
2. Make them precise and specific.
3. Write them down.
4. Refer to your list of goals frequently.
5. Then get on with it.

MEASURABLE

Assuming that your goals meet the criterion of *specific*, making them quantifiable and measurable is perfectly logical. Applying a concrete metric of measurement to your progress toward achieving them enables you to constantly evaluate yourself by an objective standard, without judgment. Did you lose three pounds this week? Did you exercise today, and for how long? Did you make three sales calls? It is critically important to develop a system for measuring your progress. Divide your goal into segments—I like about nine, falling back on my baseball analogy. Figure out a way to keep score and track your progress.

What are ways to quantify specific milestones of accomplishment, or to quantify the path to get to the "promised land" of specific goal achievement? One way is to quantify a daily time commitment toward pursuit of the goal. In Chapter 13, I discuss the tactics for task accomplishment, but you can obviously quantify the number of tasks that need to be completed to get to a goal. Part of the process of goal achievement is reducing the goal to small measurable tasks, so those tasks can be quantified and objectively completed. For example, "I will read two chapters of my chemistry book today" or "I will exercise for 60 minutes this morning." Or, on the self-denial side of the equation, "I will only consume 600 calories for lunch today." Use the analytic side of your brain to make sure the tasks you are doing to achieve your goals can be objectively measured, and you can have a clear benchmark of what needs to be accomplished in a day or a week. You can then continuously evaluate your performance achievement in relation to completing the tasks.

ACHIEVABLE

There should be some stretch to your goals, but don't make them so aggressive they are unattainable. Your goals need to be realistic and achievable for you to be successful at accomplishing them. Well-crafted goals should stretch your abilities but still remain well within the realm of possibility—even probability—of accomplishment. Setting overly optimistic or unrealistic goals will serve to discourage you on a daily basis and won't contribute to the feeling of success you experience striving to reach your goals.

From a psychological perspective, it's important to enjoy the feeling of accomplishment as you move through the process of attaining your goals. Motivationally, the difference between satisfaction and disappointment on a daily basis is both huge and emotionally dramatic. If the steps you have set for yourself are each overwhelming, you will constantly experience the disappointment of failure and you won't be encouraging yourself to move forward. There's little point in establishing goals that are so unachievable that you are psychologically intimidated as you embark on the process of trying to realize them. To be effective, your goals must be reasonably achievable. Some level of dreaming is clearly worthwhile, but there is great benefit to realism when setting goals.

There's nothing wrong with having one or two "feel good" goals that exist primarily for the psychological benefit of accomplishing them. It's good to have one or two little things that regularly contribute toward larger goals, but which are so simple that it's almost hard not to accomplish them on a daily basis. An example of this type of goal would be taking one minute every morning—*one minute*—to stop, pause, and reflect on three things you are grateful for. Or how about taking a brief time to do some form of exercise—just to force yourself to do it—in the morning? Something brief and easy like fifteen push-ups or twenty-five sit-ups. If prayer or meditation is important to you, take two or three minutes, every day, and give that time to yourself. Don't misread this paragraph: you should exercise or meditate for much longer than what I am recommending here; these are only examples of "feel good" goals that are very easy to accomplish and that can build up your psyche.

REALISTIC

The characteristic of "realistic" is quite similar to "achievable." Some writers have evolved the R in the SMART acronym to mean relevant, but to me, the notion your goals must be relevant is pretty obvious. Of course you will make sure your goals are aligned with your core values and your vision for your life, because that is what is fundamentally important to you. If you want to be a doctor, you're not going to set a goal to go to architecture school—at least not until you've made enough money to build your own office building. Regardless of how you interpret the R in the acronym, be certain your goals are realistic and relevant.

TIME-SENSITIVE

Time sensitivity brings both a certainty and a finality to goal setting, enabling you to work toward a deadline for your accomplishment. There's nothing more helpful than a deadline to make us get things done. So, establishing a time frame for accomplishing goals and tasks is essential to assuring that you will succeed in your quest to reach them. Don't set the time period for the accomplishment of particular goals so far into the future that you can't meaningfully relate to it. Deadlines shouldn't be so far off that they aren't relevant to our present lives; we need to feel the pressure of an impending cutoff date to be sure we get things done.

STRETCH GOALS

Before leaving the subject of goals and goal setting, we should consider a possible weakness of SMART goal setting: setting your sights too low and just focusing on the immediate satisfaction of task accomplishment. If you don't have any goal-setting system at all,

Chapter 10: Understanding and Establishing Goals

implementing SMART goals will increase your efficiency dramatically because the SMART system forces you to translate vague aspirations into concrete plans. However, studies have shown that people can become obsessed with achievable but inconsequential goals, losing sight of more ambitious plans. It definitely feels good to cross things off your to-do list and finish lots of projects, but it's imperative that they're worthwhile endeavors that challenge your capabilities.

In *Smarter Faster Better*,[22] Charles Duhigg details the story of the successful history of the General Electric Company's scrupulous implementation of SMART goals beginning in the late 1960s and continuing through the 1980s. Over time, however, some of GE's divisions had become unprofitable despite religious adherence to the SMART goal system. Upon careful outside review, consultants concluded that strict implementation of the SMART system caused employees to focus on inconsequential goals rather than more ambitious plans. In 1993, Jack Welch, the storied CEO of General Electric, traveled to Japan and learned of the Japanese railway system in the 1950s and the establishment of the "stretch" goal that enabled trains to go much faster than the 50 miles per hour they were then traveling. The consequence of establishing this seemingly unachievable goal was a complete overhaul of the nation's railway system: redesigned train cars, reinforced rails, rebuilt gears with less friction, and tunnels through mountains to avoid curves. The cumulative innovation that resulted from adherence to the unflinching goal of much faster trains was colossal. The result of this effort was the achievement of the Japanese bullet train traveling 120 miles per hour on its inaugural trip between Tokyo and Osaka in 1964.

---

22 Charles Duhigg, *Smarter Faster Better* (New York: Random House, 2016).

Duhigg explains that learning of Japan's success was revelatory for Welch, causing him to return to General Electric and establish audacious goals for the company moving forward. The company would need to combine the SMART system with a "stretch goal—an aim so ambitious that managers couldn't describe, at least initially, how they would achieve it."[23] The subsequent implementation of stretch goals by General Electric caused a significant overhaul of the company's processes and procedures, resulting in dramatic increases in quality and profitability. "Numerous academic studies have examined the impact of stretch goals, and have consistently found that forcing people to commit to ambitious, seemingly out-of-reach objectives can spark outsized jumps in innovation and productivity."[24]

There is definitely a balancing act to consider when adopting or enforcing stretch goals on yourself or others. There is no question that bold goals can be positively jarring and disruptive, but they can also be morale crushing. "For a stretch goal to inspire, it often needs to be paired with something like the SMART system. The reason we need both stretch goals and SMART goals is that audaciousness, on its own, can be terrifying."[25] The SMART goal system enforces an element of structure on otherwise vague intentions, and committing to a stretch goal establishes a worthwhile higher ambition. The two concepts should both be considered to achieve optimal success.

In summary, you should limit your goal development to three to five goals in alignment with your core values and the vision you have for yourself. They should follow the SMART acronym and you should adopt the practice of writing your goals and, at the

---
23 Duhigg, *Smarter Faster Better*, 125.
24 Duhigg, *Smarter Faster Better*, 126.
25 Duhigg, *Smarter Faster Better*, 127.

very least, referring back to the writing regularly. You might even consider Brian Tracy's suggestion of rewriting your goals daily for thirty days. Finally, consider adopting a meditation practice of mindfulness where you imagine yourself in the position of having achieved your goal and spending some mental energy savoring that feeling. The alternative mental trick is to imagine yourself not achieving your goal and thinking of the disappointment that that will cause you.

Mastering Self-Discipline

CHAPTER 11

MAKING GOALS ACTIONABLE:
TASKING AND TIME-ADJUSTING

Once you have undertaken the foundational steps of finding your soul (Chapter 3), developing your core values (Chapter 4), identifying your vision (Chapter 5), and the commitment step of establishing your goals (Chapter 10), you have completed the conceptual steps of the personal achievement process. However, your groundwork will lie fallow unless you convert your well-thought-out goals into a plan of execution. I call the conversion process *tasking*, and it is the process of turning your goals into concrete steps of action. Your core values and life vision led you to develop a set of goals important to your personal fulfillment. Goals are ideals, desires, and objectives, but goals don't tend to be easily "doable" steps in the process of accomplishing or achieving them; they tend to be too broad and visionary. The active steps to implement goals are *tasks*[26] and, specifically, they should be called *necessary tasks* because they are the action items that have to be implemented in order to get the job done. As a matter of fact, necessary tasks are the specific steps on which you exercise discipline (enforced personal effort). Performing necessary tasks is what makes everything happen.

---

[26] For my purposes here, the word "task" can be both a noun and a verb. A "task" (noun) is a step taken to achieve a goal. "Tasking" (verb) your goals is the process of dividing goals into manageable tasks, or steps. "You need to 'task' (verb) your goals."

Oftentimes, the missing link in the chain (the Achilles' heel, the apparent roadblock keeping you from moving forward) is the failure to properly *task* your goals into a plan of doable action that can be readily implemented in the very near term and is not so overwhelming that it causes you to be frustrated and unfulfilled. When you task your goals into a workable action plan, there are many steps you can perform in the next hour, or today, giving you emotional satisfaction because they move you forward on your life vision. If you don't task your goals into a workable plan, you won't be able to achieve success, and that failure results in frustration and the feeling that you don't have enough self-discipline to get the job done. The problem may be that you have defined the "job" too generally or too globally, such that no one could accomplish it. If you have a list of actionable items in pursuit of your well-thought-out goals and you start checking small items off your list, you will experience immediate gratification and reward for moving yourself forward. There is nothing more satisfying than finishing two or three hours of activity that, although the steps may be small, is a direct contribution toward one of the goals you seek. This is the value of learning to properly task your goals.

To use a business analogy, developing the foundation for actionable self-discipline is similar to strategic planning in a business. Strategic planning involves determining the vision and broad goals for a business: the mission statement, the grand objectives, the exit strategy for the company, etc. The actual business plan, however, lays out the detailed steps: file a fictitious name statement, write the corporate bylaws, open a bank account, set up your manufacturing process, acquire the necessary assets, hire some employees, write the software, etc. A strategic plan can be achieved, but it cannot be *done*. The steps of a business plan can be performed, executed, completed, *done*.

Chapter 11: Making Goals Actionable: Tasking and Time-Adjusting

If you task your goals into simple enough steps, you cannot fail. There is always a tiny task in pursuit of your goals that you can turn your attention to at the present moment. Because you can do that, you are always able to move yourself forward, and the result is feeling good about your immediate accomplishment. By properly tasking your goals, you are never in the frustrating position of feeling overwhelmed or incapable of advancing yourself. The key is having a menu of small steps—necessary tasks—in front of you that, when executed, contribute to your overall success.

To summarize the entire process up to this point, it is developing goals aligned with your core values and life vision and then properly tasking your goals into a lengthy laundry list of items so you can easily undertake a high-priority item (if it fits the moment) or you can choose to do an easier item. Either way, you will enjoy the psychic reward of moving the ball forward on the continuum. Failing to reduce goals to manageable tasks is where most people fall short. If your necessary tasks are well-defined, manageable and doable, it's quite enjoyable and rewarding to check them off your to-do list and, as you check little tasks off your list, you get an incredible psychic reward—regularly—for advancing the ball toward the goal.

After tasking, a second important technique contributing to making goals actionable is time-adjusting the goals. Most well-thought-out goals have a time dimension to them that is far enough in the future that it is beyond immediate reality. Given that our active lives—in terms of emotions and physical capabilities—really only consist of a present, measurable time period, it becomes important to amortize[27] your goals over a defined time period so the early parts of them can be accomplished in the near-term future.

---

27 "Amortize" is a financial term that can be defined as "spread over."

The same way you can't truly wrap your head around "becoming a doctor" if you're an eighteen-year-old, you can't realistically envision a goal that is far beyond a workable time frame. To make a goal doable, it must be reduced to a time period realistic to imagine. Stated another way, you can't effectively use a goal as a motivational tool unless you time-adjust it.

Similar to tasking, time-adjusting is another way to break down a goal, but it's dividing it into more realistic time periods. Falling back on the doctor analogy, a freshman in college can imagine herself being an orthopedic surgeon at age thirty-five and envision that goal. There is nothing wrong with a long-term goal and, for some people, that kind of goal might be motivational. However, the time-adjustment of the goal would involve dividing the vision into a time continuum and, as part of the process, bringing the goal back to or closer to the present.

For simplicity, I would suggest using the same construct for time-adjusting I used for tasking a goal, that being the analogy of a nine-inning baseball game. Take the time period of a long-term goal and divide it into nine time frames and reconceptualize the goal one-ninth of the way there, two-ninths of the way there, etc. Obviously, you can do that for any future goal and, without belaboring this fairly simple point, recognize the value of reducing the vision of the very first step of a future goal to about one month from the present.

The value of this exercise cannot be overstated. When you time-adjust a segment of a future goal to one month from now, for instance, it conforms to a time frame that enables you to appreciate both the end game (the goal) and the process (the vision) to achieve it. The emotional benefit of reducing the vision of the goal to the near-term future is very motivational, requiring much less effort to

Chapter 11: Making Goals Actionable: Tasking and Time-Adjusting

execute the tasks necessary to achieve the goal. In summary, when you combine the process of tasking your goals with time-adjusting them to a future time relatable to you, you become excited about executing necessary tasks in the next hour or the next day, and you will absolutely be on the path to success. The simple process of thinking about your future goal in incremental steps contributes to lessening the effort needed to perform the necessary tasks.

I am going to use a hypothetical example for developing a cooking class business that you can apply to identifying your own goals and reducing them to manageable tasks.

Mary Romano's core values include good nutrition, and her life vision involves helping others. Following her values and vision, she has developed a goal to start a cooking class teaching Northern Italian cooking, which happens to be a specialty of hers. She would like to accomplish her goal before December 31, six months from now. Her present job is not overwhelmingly demanding, so she has some extracurricular time on her hands and she would like to productively employ that time, do something constructive and possibly turn it into a profitable business idea.

Mary's first inquiry should be to ensure her goal is SMART. Let's evaluate it:

Specific—She plans to design, plan, market and execute a cooking class focusing on Northern Italian food. Okay, that seems pretty specific.

Measurable—She either accomplishes it or she doesn't. That seems measurable.

Achievable—There doesn't seem to be any reason Mary couldn't accomplish this goal. The goal certainly seems doable.

Realistic—Mary's desire to establish a cooking class is not overwhelmingly complicated. She is an excellent chef and she wants to share her skills with others. Her goal seems realistic. If her goal was to open a chain of Italian restaurants, that goal might be a bit unrealistic at this point in her medium-term life vision, but perhaps not later. Let's stick with the realistic goal for now, Mary.

Time-sensitive—She has a six-month time frame to accomplish her goal. That is definitely timely.

Given that Mary's desired goal passes the SMART test, the next step in the process of tasking goals is to divide the goal into nine broad task categories. (Again, there's no great reason for nine, but two or three broad categories are too few; somewhere around nine feels about right.)

1. Let's hypothesize what nine major task categories of accomplishing Mary's goal might look like.

    a. Perform general research to obtain templates of a business plan.
    b. Using the templates, prepare a preliminary outline of a plan.
    c. Investigate the existence of other classes in the city.
    d. Financial analysis and budgeting.
    e. Identify possible locations that might work for such a class.
    f. Review restaurants that might have an interest in partnering with Mary to present such a class.
    g. Research to see if there are any published materials on starting a similar business activity.
    h. Investigate whether there are any city/state regulations for operating this type of enterprise (kitchen requirements, liquor license requirements, zoning restrictions, etc.).
    i. Review and consider a handful of recipes that might work for the class.

Chapter 11: Making Goals Actionable: Tasking and Time-Adjusting

Now, we're not going to completely task Mary's goal of running a cooking class, but let's drill down on a couple of major task categories to illustrate the concept of tasking an achievable goal into minor, manageable tasks that someone could begin to perform in the very short term. I'm not suggesting you have to obsessively task out every goal in your life, but realize that reducing your goals to manageable tasks is about 80 percent of the battle of moving forward on your life vision in the near term. In my experience, one of the major stumbling blocks keeping people from exercising self-discipline is they don't have their goals divided into manageable tasks they can begin to do in small bites. It's difficult to climb an entire mountain, and it's very frustrating to imagine climbing the mountain while sitting on your couch watching football, but you can definitely take a few steps up the foothills today.

After Mary has identified the broad task categories that need to be accomplished to achieve her cooking class goal, the next step is to break them down microscopically into detailed, actionable tasks that can be completed in an hour or less. Of course, the "hour or less" time period is an ideal tasking objective that may not be workable for more complex goals, but short-term time sensitivity is a worthwhile consideration in the tasking process. Let's look at a few of Mary's task categories and divide them into microtasks:

1. Perform general research to obtain templates of a business plan.

    a. Obtain template of a generic business plan and review the categories within the plan.
    b. Schedule the areas of analysis (planning, marketing, management, budgeting, economic factors, staffing, regulations, etc.).

c. Set up a planning document for each area of necessary analysis.
   d. Identify the necessary steps of each area of the business plan.
   e. Begin drafting a generic document of the business plan for the cooking class.

2. Financial analysis and budgeting.

   a. Set up a spreadsheet program to prepare a budget for the cooking class.
   b. Identify the initial costs associated with establishing the class.
   c. Identify the costs involved with actually offering the class.
   d. For each cost analysis, vary the analysis depending on the anticipated size of the venture.
   e. Using the costs associated with starting and operating the cooking class, prepare a break-even analysis to determine the necessary revenue to break even, and to operate at a profit.
   f. Calculate the amount of capital required to undertake the venture.
   g. Assess your resources to determine if the plan is feasible.

3. Investigate the existence of other classes in the city.

   a. Search the web as a customer and see what is available.
   b. Sign up for and visit some existing classes.
   c. Evaluate the success of the other ventures.

Chapter 11: Making Goals Actionable: Tasking and Time-Adjusting

    d. Consider reaching out to other instructors/entrepreneurs to obtain information.

Enough of Mary's cooking class example. I trust you get the point of tasking a goal into actionable steps that can be completed today. The process of tasking your goals takes you from the realm of dreaming and visualizing to the nitty-gritty of actively executing the steps to accomplish your dreams. Nothing is more satisfying than doing activities in direct pursuit of your carefully considered goals. You can spend today sitting on the couch thinking about your dreams or you can do something right now to execute them—it's your choice. I know which alternative I want to pursue.

CHAPTER EXERCISE

1. Prepare a written "Goal Tasking and Time-Adjusting" document as your guide for this exercise.
2. Time-adjust the goal into a manageable time period with a conclusion as to when the goal can reasonably be achieved. Break the total period of goal achievement into a number of interim periods (deadlines) that can be used to evaluate your performance up to each of those interim time periods.
3. Divide the goal into approximately nine broad task categories and specifically identify each one.
4. Break each task category into detailed, actionable steps that can ideally be accomplished in one hour or less. Recognize some of these actionable steps may take longer, but actionable

steps should not be longer than about eight hours, at the most, and preferably much shorter.
5. For one of your goals, first analyze it to be sure it falls within the SMART goal-setting system. State the goal in the document.
6. When you have defined detailed, actionable steps that can be performed in pursuit of your goal, you have identified the action plan that you can use to move forward.

SECTION IV

PLAN OF EXECUTION FOR SELF-DISCIPLINE

CHAPTER 12

STRATEGIES FOR SELF-DISCIPLINE

SPECIFIC STRATEGIES:

Alignment
Integrity of Commitment
Effort
Understand Your Strengths and Weaknesses
Know Your Personality
Make Yourself Proud
Attitude
Live in the Present
Happiness Is Now
Disproportionate Belief in Your Capabilities
Compare Yourself to a Standard
Fantasizing versus Planning
Constant Reward
Guilt
Controlling Your Mindset Is Easier Than Controlling Your Body
Controlling Your Destiny
Developing the Habit of Self-Discipline
The Desire for Constant Self-Improvement
Use Past Success as a Basis for New Frontiers
The Character Trait of Self-Denial

One of the realities of living a self-disciplined life is learning to make yourself do tasks that, deep down, you might not want to do. Welcome to the world—you have to do the work to climb the mountain before you can enjoy the view from the peak. At a basic level, we all have to accept this reality in order to engage and move forward with our vision for ourselves. Using the tasking techniques of Chapter 11, you can make necessary tasks less burdensome by breaking them into more manageable steps, doable in the short term, and providing you with gratification from their accomplishment.

An overall strategy is a broad plan of action. Specific strategies are ways of thinking about yourself and your personal achievement process that give more meaning to the necessary tasks in front of you, making them easier to accomplish. They are conceptual frameworks that help you implement your plan of action by creating a more positive mindset toward your goals. In line with understanding your strengths and weaknesses and focusing on your strengths, it is important to know and apply specific workable strategies to your exercise of self-discipline.

In my study of self-discipline, I have discovered ways to optimize aspects of your personality style that work for you and apply those to the art of self-discipline. It is generally not productive to get down on yourself for parts of your personality or characteristics that are not working or not helping you succeed. It's important to be mindful of those faults or failings but not let them dominate your daily life, causing you to underperform or fail to achieve your goals. On the positive side, you are wise to understand and focus on aspects of your personality that will facilitate your success.

There's no question the more passionate you are about your values, vision and life purpose, the easier will be your mastery of personal discipline. The more you really want something, the harder you will work for it. If you desperately want to lose twenty pounds, it will be easier for you to forgo some calories and embark on an exercise program. If you are passionate about wanting to be a doctor, your ability to forgo a Thursday night mixer for the sake of studying organic chemistry will definitely be strengthened. Passion is a lubricating element in the process of personal achievement and the exercise of self-discipline.

ALIGNMENT

Alignment is the synchronization of your core values and vision with your goals. It is critically important for the successful practice of self-discipline. When your goals are aligned with your values and vision, executing the necessary tasks to achieve the goals becomes much easier (and it can even become effortless). Given alignment, you will be genuinely engaged in your activities and, on a good day, you can even be moving to a state of flow where you start to lose yourself in the joy of performing tasks in pursuit of your goals. Now, don't count on getting to a state of flow every day, but be aware that you can approach this level of success if you understand the deeper process. To help us get there, let's recognize some specific strategies that benefit our moving toward a state of flow.

INTEGRITY OF COMMITMENT

This strategy begins with a passionate belief in the importance of realizing your core values through the achievement of your aligned goals. Following this belief, integrity of commitment is the mental conditioning supporting your making and keeping promises to yourself. Specifically, commitment is the promise you make to yourself to perform necessary tasks to achieve your goals, and integrity is Stephen Covey's definition of the characteristic of keeping the commitment.[28] The integrity of commitment is both the promise and the follow-through execution. It requires a frame of mind that recognizes the importance of continuing on your life vision path, the significance of your immediate promise to move forward, and the integrity to honor the promise that you made.

Accomplishing something significant requires a personal commitment to yourself. The immediate challenge before you can be made easier by tasking your commitments into small, manageable steps. You can always revert to a tiny task on your fallback list and enjoy the psychological benefit of accomplishing something in pursuit of your goals. Make a commitment to yourself, honor and respect the commitment, and keep it.

EFFORT

Effort is the willingness to expend the personal energy required to perform a task or analyze a problem. Along with the integrity of commitment, it is a primary component of character. I wish I could give you an easier recipe for success, but it is only through the exercise of persistent effort that you can achieve the goals that are important to you. Mastery of self-discipline means you take the initiative to expend the effort necessary to complete the tasks to accomplish your goals. Presumably, your goals are aligned with

---
[28] Covey, *The Seven Habits of Highly Effective People*.

Chapter 12: Strategies for Self-Discipline

your values, vision and life purpose, and the alignment of those aspects of your life makes it logical—and certainly easier—to do the things you need to do.

Your ability to consistently apply personal effort to the tasks at hand is one of the most important aspects of your character. It is critical to mastering self-discipline and a key to success in your life. It doesn't matter what the motivation is for applying your individual effort, what counts is the never-ending willingness to exert yourself and keep your commitments to yourself. Carol Dweck of Stanford University says, "Effort is one of the things that gives meaning to life. Effort means you care about something, that something is important to you and you are willing to work for it. It would be an impoverished existence if you were not willing to value things and commit yourself to working toward them."[29]

Developing a habit of effort is fundamental to self-discipline and success, and the good news is personal effort can be enhanced through practice, technique and habit. One of the hacks of the process of effort is changing your attitude toward necessary tasks from neutral to positive and giving yourself gratification for accomplishing your goals. Exerting yourself in pursuit of a worthwhile task is a noble thing. Do it and enjoy it.

People who have a lot of self-discipline seem to be able to force themselves to do all kinds of things, to just suck it up and make themselves do it. Is there a way to make effort easier? Is it a habit? Is it determination? Can you visualize yourself into having an easier time with effort? The more committed you are to the core value of the goal you are pursuing, the easier the effort required to do the tasks necessary to achieve the goal. The appeal of achieving

---

29 Carol S. Dweck, *Self-Theories: Their Role in Motivation, Personality, and Development* (Philadelphia: Psychology Press, 2013), 41.

the goal becomes far more important than the undesirability of doing the necessary tasks to get there. To help yourself make necessary tasks easier, create the mental fantasy (or reality) of overweighting the value, vision and/or goal in relation to the tasks required to achieve the goal.

A simple example of this kind of motivational thinking would be a person's heavily focusing on his desire to lose twenty pounds and having that desire outweigh his immediate craving to have dessert. Think about this in a positive way because it is a very effective technique for motivating yourself. If your core values are your most deeply held beliefs and you are strongly committed to your vision to actualize your core values, doing the tasks to achieve your goals begins to move from the difficult end of the scale to the easier end of the scale.

UNDERSTAND YOUR STRENGTHS AND WEAKNESSES

"Okay, it's 3:30 on a Friday afternoon and I think I should start writing a report I need to do." (Or, "I think I should start studying for a final exam I have next Wednesday.") Seriously? Who am I kidding? It's Friday afternoon at the end of a challenging week—I am not in a state of mind to bear down and focus on something requiring that much detailed energy. Talk about a recipe for failure: forcing yourself to do one of those detailed tasks at the end of a busy week will likely result in short-term failure, resulting in disappointment.

The underlying message here is to know your strengths and weaknesses and not overexpend effort trying to fit a square peg into a round hole. Part of the mastery of self-discipline is knowing and understanding the things you are good at (and *when* you might be good at doing them) and not trying to force yourself into doing something you're likely to fail at. That doesn't mean you shouldn't challenge yourself to do things stretching your capabilities—you should—but don't foolishly try to do things that don't fit into your wheelhouse.

Another thing to keep in mind about the "Friday afternoon syndrome" is you should have something worthwhile to invest in during the less productive time that inevitably occurs. Just because a particular time slot isn't prime time for your maximum productivity doesn't mean you should waste the time snacking, playing solitaire or surfing the internet. Your fallback list should include some productive tasks you ought to be doing during your less productive time windows. Maybe return some easier phone calls or emails, or contact an acquaintance to arrange a get-together—something that better fits with the reality of life at the moment. Focus on your strengths and minimize your weaknesses.

KNOW YOUR PERSONALITY

Having an understanding of yourself is key to being able to successfully negotiate the day (or hour) in front of you. What aspects of your personality can you exploit to help you accomplish the tasks necessary to achieve your goals? Try to identify your particular character traits that will enable you to be successful so you capitalize on your strengths and minimize your weaknesses. Be aware of the inefficiency of trying to "force it" too much: it simply won't work.

Depending on your personality, your best strategy may be competing with yourself (or someone else) to get something done. One of the first people I interviewed for my research for this book was a woman named Stephanie Hawkins, a successful professional whose serious avocation is competitive martial arts.[30] When I asked her what she relied on to motivate herself, her answer was competing with an imaginary other person. It didn't matter if it was her hobby or other aspects of her life: she was deeply competitive, and that was what she used to drive her success. She would imagine if she didn't do an immediate necessary task, not only would she not accomplish what she needed to, but she would fall doubly behind because the mythical "other fighter" would step up to the plate and do what was necessary, and that would put Stephanie two steps behind her imaginary competitor. If she didn't accomplish the next thing on her to-do list, the other person would do it and would gain a point, and she would lose a point, down by a total of two. For her, competition is the motivator.

What are the aspects of your personality that will help you accomplish the necessary tasks of the day? For me, for example, it's having the necessary tasks broken into small enough bites so I can easily achieve the psychological benefit of accomplishing success. I can't bear to force myself to sit down to do something that's going to take hours and hours to accomplish—that simply won't mesh with my attention span, so I need to have manageable bites to chew on. Maybe your personality need is quiet concentration, or socialization with others, or checking things off your list. Surely there are things about yourself you are in touch with that motivate you. Recognize what they are and use them as the basis for designing your immediate plan for the next hour of your day.

---
30 Not Stephanie's real last name.

Chapter 12: Strategies for Self-Discipline

MAKE YOURSELF PROUD

Pride and disappointment are two sides of the same coin we flip about every ten minutes of our lives. No matter what we do, one side of the coin will turn up. If your actions in that ten-minute time segment are in alignment with your values, vision and life purpose, you will feel proud of yourself for pursuing important activities. If you are not advancing your life purpose, you will feel disappointment.

I remember reading a book by Christopher Reeve, the acclaimed actor who was critically injured in an equestrian accident and lived for nine years after his injury as a respiratory quadriplegic. He wrote several books and became a beacon of light for his readers and fans. I remember his description of morality, which went something like this: "When I do good, I feel good, and when I do bad, I feel bad." That comment always seemed to be a meaningful barometer to me because it identifies the most basic human emotion everyone wants to experience—feeling good. We all want to feel good about ourselves and feel proud of our life's direction and accomplishments. There is nothing wrong with using pride in your bag of tricks as a motivator for yourself to advance your cause. Be positive about yourself. You have that choice this minute, and you shouldn't squander it.

ATTITUDE

Speaking of choice, at any moment in time, your attitude is a choice. How you contemplate something you are about to do falls on a spectrum of choices. You have the choice to think positively or negatively about the next activity you are undertaking. How you choose to think about it dramatically changes the energy required to perform the task in front of you. And, you can change your attitude toward the task—*immediately.*

This morning I am going to the pool to swim my half mile. I have the choice to think positively or negatively about my activity, and the difference between those two mindsets completely affects the experience of my exercise routine. I can dread it and think about how hard it's going to be or how it interrupts my lazy morning. Or, I can create the fantasy of the healthy body I am creating for myself and how my exercise contributes to that. I can also think about the parts of the exercise I truly enjoy. For me, it's my body sliding through the cool water or the intermittent bursting and relaxing of the exercise (I particularly enjoy the relaxing part!).

The important point of the concept of managing your attitude is that switching mental gears on how you think about a necessary task is very easy, and it should be part of your self-discipline routine. The mental framework by which you approach some task—possibly even an unpleasant one—radically affects the level of effort required to perform the task. Which level of effort would you prefer to have to expend to perform an important task? The answer is obvious and the strategy is a no-brainer. You simply have to manage your mindset. Positive attitude—put your mind in a state of certainty about yourself, your abilities, and your commitment to your goals. Decide, commit, resolve.

When you think about managing your attitude, be aware of the data on the effect of changing your mental attitude by simply altering your physical state. Many years ago I attended a weekend program given by Tony Robbins and, among many other things, he said he never asks someone *why* they feel bad. He would always ask them *how* they feel bad. The implication of his comment was that the person who feels bad invariably has poor posture, a sad look on his face, and a generally depressed affect about himself. The first step to curing a poor mental attitude is to change your physical state by correcting physical posture and putting a positive expression on your face. Even if you're fooling yourself into a positive attitude, it's a wonderful place to start. And, believe it or not, it works!

LIVE IN THE PRESENT

Remember, life is a journey, not a destination. The only mindset you have is in the present, and the choice of your emotional state (happiness, sadness, worry, or anxiety) is only a condition existing right now. You can't be happy (or sad) tomorrow. You can only experience an emotion right now.

Micromanaging your mindset means realizing the only time you have to be productive, be real, be yourself, to actually *live* is now and in the immediate future, like the next hour or so of your life. To carry this concept to a ridiculous degree, maybe the only time you really have is thirty or sixty seconds, but the thought of that is a little extreme. But, micromanaging that machine—that "you," that mind and body—is the key to everything in life. Living in *this* reality, realizing that pursuing your core values, your goals, your purpose—*right now*—is the key to happiness.

When you live in the present, you become aware of the negative ramifications of the mental habits of worrying, beating yourself up, feeling inadequate or stewing in other destructive thoughts. There is very little upside to those thought processes and, to the extent they take away from your focus on the present and what you can do in the next hour of your life, they undermine your progress. Lose the negativism and concentrate on what you can do right now to contribute to your core values and goals. Don't waste the next hour of your life—it's the only hour that you ever have.

HAPPINESS IS NOW

The concept of happiness is very much in the same vein as living in the present. Happiness is doing things presently in pursuit of your aligned goals. We all want to be on a path to fulfilling our purpose in life, but we need to realize happiness is simply *being* on the path of that purpose-driven life and life is the journey, not the destination. The destination is imaginary; the path is real. The reality is that happiness is only now, not tomorrow. Hopefully you will also be happy tomorrow, but you can't experience that happiness until then. Don't sacrifice any of your present happiness by worrying about how you might feel tomorrow. You can only "feel" today.

DISPROPORTIONATE BELIEF IN YOUR CAPABILITIES

No one ever achieves success without believing they can succeed, regardless of what anyone around them says. While no one can guarantee you will achieve your goals, you can be assured

Chapter 12: Strategies for Self-Discipline

you won't exceed your goals, unless you win the lottery. So the logical approach to life is to set high goals for yourself and force the belief you can attain them. There is virtually no downside to this strategy, only upside. I am not suggesting you live a life of delusion, but the benefits of thinking optimistically about yourself and your possibilities far outweigh the burden of thinking negatively about yourself. Get out of any funk you allow yourself to devolve into and get with the positive program.

COMPARE YOURSELF TO A STANDARD

The practice of self-comparison can either be motivating or deflating. Some people thrive on striving for something better than themselves, and for them, having a target to reach for is a positive influence on their ability to move forward. Others choose to compare themselves to something worse so they are always winning, and a third group compares themselves to an equal so they are always competing. How you apply this strategy of self-discipline is up to you; just be aware of the alternatives and their effect on you.

Using self-comparison can be an effective technique to motivate yourself to do the necessary tasks to achieve your goals. It can also be a hindrance to moving yourself forward, because you can find yourself in a situation of always failing at your goals if you're comparing yourself to an unachievable standard. Of course, this is fine for people who have the psychological need to always be striving and for whom constant striving is a positive motivating factor. On the other hand, I personally don't like always failing or never achieving the goals of the day, whether they are big or small. I have occasionally found myself failing to move forward on a task because I have set such a high standard for myself that it is somewhat disappointing to try to move forward with a task that is very difficult for me to succeed at. If you're going to go out and hit a few tennis balls and you constantly compare yourself to Roger Federer, it doesn't feel very good—at least for me. I don't like the feeling of always being behind. That may be a motivator for some people but it is a deflator for me.

Spend a little time evaluating the type of personality you have in this regard and gravitate toward the self-comparison model that boosts your personal motivation. Simply being aware of these different comparison metrics enables you to think about the style that supports you, and you can use that knowledge to better manage your mental state.

FANTASIZING VERSUS PLANNING

Fantasy is a procrastination mechanism. It's not programming your brain for what you are doing (for today or the next hour); it's programming your brain to do nothing other than dream about what some part of you thinks you should do, and it allows you to do nothing in the moment. You climb mountains one step at a time, and if you sit around dreaming about the mountain you want to climb, or you should climb, or you ought to climb, then you're not taking the next step—even if it's a baby step—and you're never going to climb the mountain. You're going to spend your time *thinking* about climbing the mountain.

There's nothing wrong with planning; in fact, it is critically important. But there's a difference between planning and fantasizing. Planning is similar to tasking, and it is the affirmative act of detailing the steps necessary to achieve a goal, whether it's a short-term goal like planning for an effective day or week, or a long-term goal such as completing an educational degree or starting a business. Planning is contemplating and documenting the specific steps (tasks) you have to undertake to accomplish a goal. Fantasizing is dreaming about the future. Dreaming has a place in life, and I don't want to suggest you should never engage in it, but be aware of the difference and consider evolving your dreams into goals and goals into detailed plans (tasks).

CONSTANT REWARD

Another effective way to motivate yourself is through the success pattern of constant rewards. Break your goals into necessary tasks, especially very small ones, and reward yourself for the success of completing each task. If your goal is to learn a foreign language, for example, there are many obvious steps to achieve the goal, and you could set up a vision (or plan) with many little steps you can reward yourself for upon completion of each one. The psychological benefit of little successes is cumulative, and those successes create both momentum and positive inertia. It's analogous to a pattern of forming good habits.

GUILT

The opposite of motivating yourself through a reward system is motivation by good old-fashioned guilt. You just force yourself to do things you don't particularly want to do because you are convinced they are the right thing to do, and you feel terrible if you don't do them. For some people, guilt is a worthless emotion that has no value in their lives, but others find it motivating. Since getting the job done is of paramount importance, if guilt works for you, by all means use it. That particular motivational strategy has never worked very well for me because I don't have a strong sense of irrational duty. I need to have a reason to want to do things I should do, and "My mother always said I should" just doesn't really work for me. But if guilt works for you, use it to get the job done.

CONTROLLING YOUR MINDSET IS EASIER THAN CONTROLLING YOUR BODY

Controlling your body (your tasks, your effort, your self-denial) is hard, but supervising your mindset is easy. If you learn the relatively effortless technique of managing your mindset, it's much easier to apply self-discipline to your actions. Think of it as controlling the next thirty seconds of your mental life. What could be easier? You can easily micromanage your mindset to control your attitude right now and expand that control to your physical activities for the next hour. (You can do anything for an hour, can't you? Studying, push-ups, laundry, cleaning the kitchen, mowing the lawn—just about anything, right?)

Managing your mindset is a foundational key to the whole process. Self-discipline over your thinking is as simple as changing your attitude. You control your attitude every moment. You can make it positive and peaceful or you can make it negative

Chapter 12: Strategies for Self-Discipline

and stressed. I have concluded that one of the easiest life hacks is a mental one. I fully recognize it is easier to think about doing things than it is to actually do them, but thinking about them is the first step in the process. You have the power to step back, take a few deep breaths, and put yourself into a positive frame of mind toward the next short period of your life. You control your thought process every moment, and you can evolve it into a positive feeling or a negative feeling.

At any moment, you have the power to replace a negative thought with a positive thought, regardless of what is going on around you. External realities happen to all of us and we cannot control them, but we always have the power to control the way we react to situations.

CONTROLLING YOUR DESTINY

There's just something good about the feeling of being in charge instead of being pushed around. I don't know anyone who relishes the latter situation. Much of control is just a momentary mental attitude adjustment: you control the situation or it controls you. In the immediate moment, the concept of control is the feeling of being slightly ahead of the curve and using the power of momentum to help propel you as opposed to being behind the curve and constantly fighting to catch up.

You have the power to direct the course of your life, and again, back to baby steps, even if it's only for the next thirty minutes, the difference between having your body work for you (your Being) and the opposite of that, which is being a slave to anything—your situation, your job, another person, whatever—is remarkable. It feels good to be in control of your life, and you have the power to establish that control, at least in a psychological way, almost all the time.

In order to be in control of your life, focus on the moment, not your entire lifetime. If you use the skill of properly tasking and time-adjusting your goals, you will identify doable steps in front of you, enabling you to be ahead of the curve and in control of your situation. Alternatively, if you allow yourself to be overwhelmed because the tasks in front of you are overwhelmingly difficult or time consuming, you are allowing the situation to control you.

DEVELOPING THE HABIT OF SELF-DISCIPLINE

The habit of applying self-discipline to small tasks is its own strategy of self-discipline. Forcing yourself to do little tasks you don't particularly want to do builds the character traits of self-control and self-regulation and is very helpful in developing the larger habit of self-discipline. Habits are recurring patterns of behavior, and our brains operate on habit about 95 percent of the time. They are patterns we fall into for survival and, for both good and bad, we have the power to shape our habits. Experts say a habit can be established (or replaced with another habit) within three to four weeks of consistent activity. In the course of researching and writing this book, I have developed a number of positive habits that have significantly changed my life for the better. For example, I previously mentioned I have established a keystone habit of religiously doing a very brief exercise routine every morning before I do anything else, and it creates a "checked-off-the-list" feeling of satisfaction that energizes me for the day.

Chapter 12: Strategies for Self-Discipline

THE DESIRE FOR CONSTANT SELF-IMPROVEMENT

The Japanese philosophy of constant improvement is known as kaizen, the practice of continuous improvement in your personal and professional life. The most basic premise of kaizen philosophy is to institute incremental improvements over time for the betterment of the whole. It is a complete life philosophy about which much is written,[31] but in its most summary fashion, it involves living with a vision of life as a work in process composed of continuous small improvements. If you view every hour of your day as an opportunity to do better than you did before, it is obvious you will constantly evolve into your better self, and your quest to achieve your core values and vision will be fulfilled. I keep a little handwritten sign on my bathroom mirror that asks, "Did I do better today than yesterday?"

USE PAST SUCCESS AS A BASIS FOR NEW FRONTIERS

We all have areas of our lives in which we are or have been very successful performers. These areas can be analyzed to become the basis for successfully moving forward. This strategy of self-discipline involves getting in touch with those experiences and identifying the feelings that drove them as well as the feelings that resulted from the successful accomplishment of the activities. With some creative thinking and planning, you can use the emotional experience from these past successes to craft ways to

---

31 http://www.kaizenvision.com/start-here/

perform present necessary tasks in light of the good feelings you have experienced from performing past activities.

This technique isn't a perfect remedy for accomplishing difficult tasks, but when it is used with other strategies and tactics of self-discipline, it lightens the load of the current tasks before you. As an exercise, think of four or five things you have done in the past that you truly enjoyed doing. Focus on one of those activities and identify the feelings you got from engaging in that desirable activity. Now try to frame necessary current tasks in the context of the positive feelings you are in touch with and think about ways to perform these current tasks in light of those feelings.

Recall that one of the best definitions of happiness is presently doing tasks in pursuit of your goals, and try to think about ways to visualize a current, necessary task—perhaps an unpleasant one—in a positive light in terms of your goals or purpose in life. The motivation to perform necessary tasks is based on your desire to advance your guiding principles. Try to constantly reframe your perspective about each necessary task through the lens of your core values, your goals and your purpose in life.

THE CHARACTER TRAIT OF SELF-DENIAL

Just having this character trait in your bag of tricks is powerful as a strategy for self-discipline. Learning to say no to yourself is good practice for developing and enhancing your powers of self-control. One of my personal guiding principles is "My Being controls my body," and forcing my body to obey my Being reinforces the principle and builds the habit of discipline. You don't have to do it all the time, of course, but learning to say no to yourself for the right things is a very good habit to develop.

Chapter 12: Strategies for Self-Discipline

SUMMARY OF STRATEGIES FOR SELF-DISCIPLINE

1. Reflect on whether your goals are in alignment with your core values and your life vision, and work to be sure they are synchronous.
2. Be certain you are committed to expending a consistent level of effort to achieve your goals.
3. Work diligently to develop a habit of effort in everything productive you do.
4. Evaluate your personal strengths and weaknesses and focus your efforts on the necessary tasks that most closely fit your personality style. Delegate incompatible tasks to others.
5. Understand the motivating force behind your personality and focus on that force as a basis for moving forward. Are you competitive? Driven? Afraid of failure? Use that force to your advantage.
6. Savor the feeling of personal pride as you execute tasks in pursuit of your goals.
7. Recognize you have the ability to choose a positive or a negative attitude toward the necessary tasks before you, and they are infinitely easier if you approach them with positivity.
8. Your only emotional existence is in the present and your emotional state is a present choice. Manage your present mindset in a positive way.
9. Happiness is doing present tasks in pursuit of your aligned goals.
10. Believe in your capability to achieve your well-thought-out goals.

11. Use the concept of comparing yourself to a standard (competing, striving, or exceeding) as a basis for self-motivation.
12. Be aware that dreaming can be a procrastination mechanism and work to convert your dreams into goals and your goals into necessary tasks.
13. Break your necessary tasks into small steps and reward yourself for the success of completing each task.
14. Manage your mindset: replace negative thoughts with positive ones.
15. Stay ahead of the curve. Make the mental adjustment to be in control of the next hour of your life rather than allowing it to control you.
16. Develop the habit of self-discipline: force yourself to regularly do small, routine tasks contributing to your goals and benefiting you.
17. Practice kaizen, the Japanese philosophy of constant improvement.
18. Rely on your past successful experiences as a psychological basis for new frontiers.
19. Practice saying no to yourself to stop behaviors that don't contribute to your core values.

CHAPTER 13

TACTICS FOR TASK ACCOMPLISHMENT

Act now, for now is all you have.
—Og Mandino

INTRODUCTION

GENERAL TACTICS:

- Keystone Habits
- Baby Steps: An Immediate Way of Thinking
- Little Victories
- Deadlines
- Accountability
- Visualization
- Frame Tasks in a Positive Light
- Time Management, Scheduling, Planning, and Reviewing
- Self-Control and Self-Denial
- Don't Negotiate with Yourself

DAILY TACTICS:

- Morning Routine
- Reviewing Your Day and Setting Up Tomorrow
- Weekly Commitments

Daily Tracking Sheet
Quick Review and Reset Ritual
Identify the Time Period That Works for You
Organizing
Do Two Things instead of One
Doing the Next Best Thing

Goals are specific milestones in your life that are accomplished or achieved. They are medium- to long-term intentions you have chosen to help you realize your core values and life vision. Generally, goals are longer-range objectives than the types of things on your daily to-do list. In contrast to goals, tasks are the chores (jobs, duties, work, things requiring effort) that have to be completed to accomplish goals. They are today's items that need to get done. By analogy, tasks are the push-ups you have to do to get in physical condition. Physical condition is the goal; push-ups are the work to get there. Everyone knows you can't get to the goal without expending the effort to do the necessary tasks to get there.

Tasks can either be affirmative actions you must undertake to achieve your goals or, negatively, they are the forbearance of activities that are counterproductive toward your goals. Affirmative tasks, or necessary tasks, range on a scale of desirability from loathed to enjoyable. There are some necessary tasks we just hate to do, and we use all the tricks of procrastination, distraction, prioritization, denial, and others to avoid doing them. They are our least desirable activities. How many times have you finally completed an undesirable necessary task and realized you spent more energy avoiding the task than actually doing it? It's embarrassing to even think about it, but we've all done it.

Chapter 13: Tactics for Task Accomplishment

And then there are the forbearance activities, the "negative tasks" essential in the world of self-discipline. These are the sacrifices requiring self-denial to stop wasting time, eat less, stop smoking, stop drinking to excess, stop gambling, and avoid some of life's vices that can be pleasurable but that need to be reined in. Self-denial is as much a component of one side of self-discipline as effort and self-motivation are components of the other side of it.

Self-discipline is the ability to exert personal control and command over yourself to make you do tasks that are necessary, but may be less than enjoyable, to get where you want to be. Conversely, self-discipline is also the ability to forgo doing things that are desirable on some level but don't contribute to your overall core values. If we could all just consistently enforce a high level of self-discipline on ourselves, our lives could approach perfection. We would accomplish everything we dream of and we would rid ourselves of any bad habits that haunt us. We would all be powerful, rich, and most importantly, in Olympic physical condition.

Again I ask you to step back for a minute and contemplate the following thought: the next hour of your life is the only life you really have. Your past is history and the future is a fantasy. You don't really *have* to do anything; you can change your attitude and *choose* to do the tasks you should do to achieve your goals. Discipline is living this hour, making this next hour productive and experiencing the true happiness of doing tasks in pursuit of your goals, your purpose and your passion. If the task in front of you is unpleasant, compare the immediate pain of the self-discipline of doing the task to the pain of regretting you didn't do it.

By positively committing to the next hour of your life, you get the joy of the triple reward by which (1) you work toward accomplishing your outcome goal, (2) you don't go a step backward, and (3) you get the bonus of the psychic benefit of advancing your life vision. If you make the determination that everything you do in the next hour is going to add value to your overall purpose in life, you have changed the notion that the tasks before you are monumental, and now one or two of them, at least, are manageable in the next hour. And, think about the converse of that positive commitment: there is a deficit created by everything you do that doesn't add value to your purpose, and that deficit is antithetical to the person you are.

This chapter focuses on the tactics that can be employed to make necessary tasks easier to perform and forbearance easier to withstand. There are some relatively simple tactics to make today a great day and the next hour of your life a positive experience. Think of them as a menu of tactics, some or all of which will work for you and help you achieve your desired goals.

GENERAL TACTICS:
KEYSTONE HABITS

Rather than overwhelm yourself with the idea of having self-discipline in everything you do or every task you undertake, a very effective beginning tactic is to force yourself to be disciplined in one or two small but important areas. This is an application of the concept of reducing your life vision to manageable bites so you're not intimidated by all the things you have to do to achieve all of your goals. Finding one or two little things you consistently do will anchor your mind (and body) into a pattern of self-discipline you can use as a basis to bring about larger change in your life. Charles Duhigg, author of *The Power of Habit,* calls these small but important patterns "keystone habits."[32] Keystone habits don't create a direct cause-and-effect relationship, but they can spark "chain reactions that help other good habits take hold," Duhigg writes.

Keeping a very organized workspace is an example of a keystone habit or a single area in which the exercise of self-discipline can have significant ramifications. And, it's not an overwhelming task to accomplish. The simple act of cleaning up your desk at the beginning of your workday (or the end, or both) is a pretty easy task to regularly check off your list. Another example of a keystone habit to begin significant change in your life is weighing yourself every day if you're trying to lose weight. It's not difficult to force yourself to undertake this task, and the religious adherence to this simple little habit will have very beneficial consequences to your overall self-discipline practice. A third example is a commitment to a simple exercise routine you do religiously every morning. Now, for this keystone habit, I really do mean a simple routine that takes less than three to five minutes. For starters, try twenty push-ups or twenty-five sit-ups, or whatever level of very brief basic exercise fits your conditioning. The effect of this keystone habit is to ground yourself to a basic commitment you keep religiously and you mentally reward yourself for.

One of the benefits of adopting and practicing these small keystone habits is they allow you to experience the feeling of success, even if it's only in a small way. Our minds are easily conditioned, and they can be conditioned to success or failure. The benefit of

---

32 Charles Duhigg, *The Power of Habit: Why We Do What We Do in Life and Business* (New York: Random House Trade, 2012), 109.

practicing keystone habits or baby steps of self-discipline is they create the habit of success, and that habit is contagious in our lives. Success feels good and it is habit-forming.

BABY STEPS: AN IMMEDIATE WAY OF THINKING

A technique similar to keystone habits is the concept of breaking your life up into manageable bites. Here, we are dealing with two critically important time segments of our lives: the important *mental* segment is the next thirty to sixty seconds and the important *physical* segment is the next thirty to sixty minutes. Sometimes I discuss them interchangeably, but I think you'll get the picture.

You can break the next hour of your life into a manageable situation for yourself, recognizing your personality strengths, and move forward with the hour (the only hour of your life you really have control of) in a positive way that contributes to your core values and beliefs. If you do that, you will be happy, right now, in real time, controlling the physical aspect of your life. On the mental side of things, if you don't micromanage your mindset (the next sixty seconds), you can let all kinds of other "demons" control you—things like negative thoughts, the "what ifs," the jealousy of others, the anger toward others or things that are outside of your life and you can't control anyway. It's important to realize the tendencies to fall into negative self-talk and worry, and negativism sucks the positive energy out of your brain.

So, it's a little overly simplistic (but true) to say your entire life is a choice, but it isn't so overwhelming to think the next very short period of life is a choice. (Let's call it one minute for the sake of

Chapter 13: Tactics for Task Accomplishment

discussion.) And, first and foremost, you can control your mindset for this minute. Positive or negative. (How easy is that?) Don't waste time thinking about yesterday or tomorrow. There is nothing wrong with reminiscing about things from the past, but there is a difference between enjoying positive memories and stewing over something bad that happened to you. Remember, nine times out of ten, there is nothing you can do about the bad memory, and dwelling on it is not contributing anything to your well-being.

And, with regard to contemplating your future, long-term planning is a very necessary and productive exercise to undertake. But there is a difference between planning your future and fantasizing that your life will be wonderful when X is accomplished, attained or received. Make sure you are not wasting valuable current energy on daydreaming about the future when you would be better off investing your energy in the necessary tasks to achieve your goals.

Everybody knows it's a challenging mental exercise to contemplate climbing a majestic mountain peak, but it's not difficult to think about taking the first step or even walking a few hundred yards up the foothill. We all have thousands of thoughts every day, and you can only focus on one thought at a time, and a good, positive thought can be used to replace a negative thought. Given that our entire mental experience is in the immediate present, you can use an easy mental baby step to presently control your destiny.

By taking control of the present mental minute, you acquire the power to control your physical actions for the next relatively short period of time, which I estimate to be about one hour. For those of us with stronger attention spans, the control period may be longer, and that's great. But the starting place is getting positive control of your immediate mental mindset.

So, think about this: you're not dealing with losing weight, stopping smoking, getting a new job or making your life entirely different; you're only dealing with the next short period of your life and whether or not you want to feel good about it for about sixty minutes. This microcosmic approach to living is very beneficial because it focuses you on a workable segment of your life. Your Being can work on the management of larger segments of your life (goal setting, planning, long-term vision, life purpose), but your body is only involved with the present. You can only really act *now*.

LITTLE VICTORIES

The concept of little victories involves getting out of your head and ridding yourself of the many negative thoughts we carry with us and stew over. They are not productive, and they rob us of the peaceful, positive stride that is essential to moving ourselves forward. To be successful on the path of personal achievement, you must replace negative thoughts with a fallback list of manageable tasks that is fairly short and consists of tiny tasks, including things you can do almost anywhere or anytime. The fallback list isn't the place where you keep track of your "big steps"; it really has to be the little victories you can achieve with minimal effort. The result of achieving little victories brings you the psychological satisfaction of moving toward the accomplishment of your goals.

In the category of negative thoughts are the "shoulds, coulds and wish-I-hads." One of the natural patterns of our brains is to drop into the "shoulda-coulda-wish-I-had" mindset that saps our mental energy. Think about it—what good does that type of negative thinking do for us? Absolutely nothing. First of all, it takes us out of the present, which is the only time we can do anything about these thoughts. Second, it creates disappointment and discouragement from feeling bad about not accomplishing something. There is no value to obsessing about something you should do in the future or something you didn't do in the past. To contrast that negative way of thinking, bring yourself to the present and immediately contemplate (or do) something to remedy the situation.

Think of a list of "shoulds": lose ten pounds, get in shape, quit smoking, connect with friends, write an article; there are hundreds of things people walk around thinking they "should" do. One of the ways you can change the story about something you are stewing over is to break the "should" or the dream into a goal and then into such small baby steps you can easily and regularly accomplish one or two of them. For example, if you "should" quit smoking, you can replace the smoke break you take at 10:15 a.m. with a healthy walk around the block. (Yeah, I know it isn't entirely that simple, but I can keep you from having one cigarette with this little victory.) Then, focus on the psychological reward you are rightfully entitled to for accomplishing one little victory. Life is the accumulation of your accomplishments, and if your actions are in pursuit of your well-thought-out goals, you will be a very satisfied person. Little victories resulting from necessary tasks will contribute significantly to your success.

DEADLINES

Nothing is more effective for completing a task than a deadline, especially one involving another person. For years, I have observed professionals—particularly lawyers, because they have been my clients—working on significant cases, and the "committee" always seems to be very comfortable using any excuse to kick the task completion can down the road. But, when there is a real deadline, particularly one imposed by a judge, it is amazing what gets accomplished at the eleventh hour before the deadline.

There is a practical benefit to making a commitment to another person to complete a task by a deadline. In effect, we have promised something, and we don't want to break the promise or let the other person down. Even if the other person isn't invested in the activity (i.e., it doesn't benefit him or her), just the fact we have told them we will accomplish X by 5:00 p.m. on Wednesday is significant. Some people are the type who start working on the college term paper after the first class of the semester, but those generally aren't the folks who are reading this book. The rest of us need the professor's deadline to get the paper done. Let's face reality—we need to use all the tricks and tactics we can to complete necessary tasks. Tell a friend you will do X by 5:00 p.m. on Wednesday and you'll be cramming to get it done. Who cares? Use whatever it takes to get the job done. Create a deadline.

ACCOUNTABILITY

The concept of accountability creates a responsibility that weighs on you and makes it easier to accomplish the tasks you have identified as necessary to achieving your goals. It would be great if we all could hold ourselves accountable directly to ourselves for everything in our lives, but the reality is that it's sometimes more effective to involve another person to be responsible to. Don't be embarrassed or ashamed to involve another person in your application of accountability—a friend or even a professional life coach—whatever it takes to get the job done is A-OK.

Chapter 13: Tactics for Task Accomplishment

Although it is definitely helpful to share your current goals with a few other people close to you—respected colleagues or significant others—be prepared for those people to argue against your plan. Listen carefully to their criticism and incorporate any valuable comments into your thinking, but don't allow yourself to be discouraged by anyone's lack of complete support for your quest. People can be negative or even jealous of your plan, and it is important you consider what they have to say as constructive criticism but not be discouraged by their views.

Also, there are techniques to apply accountability in your daily life. For most of my professional career, I was the managing principal of a professional services firm similar to a law firm or an accounting firm. We required ourselves to account for our professional time every day for the purpose of billing our clients. What I learned from that reality is that keeping track of your working time increases your efficiency dramatically. One of my few absolute requirements as the firm's manager was that every professional had to turn in a time sheet every day, and there was no allowance to defer the preparation of the time sheet to the end of the week. In fact, there are studies showing that weekly, as opposed to daily, preparation of time sheets in professional firms reduces the accumulation of billable time by as much as 30 percent from daily accountability of employees' time. So, accounting for your time every day with some mechanism can be very helpful to your efficiency.

VISUALIZATION

Another very effective tactic of task completion is visualization. It is a technique that sets up your subconscious mind for success and achievement. Simply stated, visualization is the process of mentally experiencing every sensation of the completed task. It's the technique of using your imagination to create and visualize scenarios in your mind's eye. You create a mental image and then focus on the image for a period of time. You see yourself in the situation you want to be in and you try to imagine all the physical sensations of being there. There is no question the technique is used by successful people—particularly athletes or others accomplishing physical feats—to help them accomplish their goals.

Create a detailed scenario of your task or goal. If you are visualizing a short-term task, imagine the feeling of accomplishment you will experience in an hour or two if you invest the necessary energy and engagement to attend to the task at hand. If your visualization exercise is for a longer-term goal, imagine the details of the future situation—very specifically—down to the physical location, the people around you, the way you would dress and carry yourself, the home you would live in, and the car you would drive. Fill in the blanks with what is important to you: it may be relationship-oriented or material acquisitions—whatever is meaningful to you. But make sure your visualization process is in the present tense, seeing yourself *in* the situation where you want to be, not planning or hoping to be there. Visualization is a current mental exercise, not a future fantasy. Among other benefits, visualization sets your subconscious mind on the path to accomplishment of the tasks or goals ahead of you.

FRAME TASKS IN A POSITIVE LIGHT

There are many undesirable necessary tasks. Hopefully, you have tasked the steps toward your goal so they are manageable and time-adjusted, but now an excellent technique to assist in

Chapter 13: Tactics for Task Accomplishment

task completion is to frame the undesirable tasks in a more positive light. Use your creativity to convert tasks into fun activities. For instance, maybe you can do this honestly with yourself by turning exercising into a game of tennis or you can make going to the gym a fun game. Now, I am not naïve about the difficulty of some of these techniques; I am just trying to offer every possible tactic to make the exercise of task accomplishment easier.

There is no question it's easy to do what you want to do, but it's harder to do what you have to do. The trick is to learn how to turn the things you have to do into things you want to do. You can make tasks more enjoyable by changing your attitude toward them, dividing tasks into shorter time periods, and/or playing games with them. The more passionate you are about the vision for your life, the more excited you will be about performing the tasks to achieve the goals of the vision.

TIME MANAGEMENT, SCHEDULING, PLANNING, AND REVIEWING

The term "time management" is actually a misnomer because we can't manage time; we can only manage ourselves and our relationship with time. I am always amazed that we all have the same amount of time, but some of us manage to accomplish enormous things with the time we have while others of us just stumble along. The experts in time management strategies suggest you cannot manage time; you manage the events in your life in relation to time.[33]

---

[33] Sue W. Chapman and Michael Rupured, "Ten Strategies for Better Time Management," May 2008, University of Georgia Cooperative Extension, https://docplayer.net/284753-Time-management-10-strategies-for-better-time-management-sue-w-chapman-michael-rupured-know-how-you-spend-your-time.html.

As defined by Wikipedia, time management is a form of self-monitoring using time as the regulator and the observer of time (you) as the governor. The first aspect of time management is the organization of the tasks you must perform to accomplish your goals. A simple ABC methodology is sufficient, or the more compulsive student of time management might prioritize tasks both in importance and urgency. Obviously, you will focus on the higher-priority items before the lower ones and, critically, you should implement a scheduling technique to accomplish your daily tasks. You should be mindful to minimize interruptions, because they break your flow of task accomplishment, and be aware of the tendency to multitask. Multitasking feels efficient, but the evidence suggests it isn't.

In my experience, scheduling is an important aspect of time management. Everyone has some form of prioritizing the necessary tasks required to accomplish short-term (or long-term) goals, but a prioritized list is meaningless unless you've actually taken a few minutes to schedule blocks of time to perform the tasks on the list. Scheduling is an incredibly effective tool, and as soon as you start doing it, you'll ask yourself why it took you so long to figure this out. If something is important enough to put on your list, it is important enough to carve out a block of time to do it. If you don't schedule your tasks, making a list is like adding a stone to your backpack. You can go through life continually adding stones to your backpack, but pretty soon you're going to be carrying around a heavy burden. You obviously have to have a mechanism to get the stones off your back, and scheduling a specific time to perform necessary tasks is the perfect mechanism.

The simple reality is that planning and organizing your day, your week, your month, and your year will change your level of productivity exponentially. Bearing down on the present, you have a precious day in front of you. As I've said over and over, it's the only day you'll ever really have. Shouldn't you take a few minutes in the morning and think about how you are going to invest this day, these twelve or fourteen hours? You know if you just let the day happen to you or control you, you won't make the most of it. You also know you can take charge of it, organize it, and design how you are going to use it.

There is no correct way to manage time that works for everyone. Some folks use a calendar to schedule planned actions, others use to-do lists and a method of prioritization to ensure things get done. The important thing is taking the time, proactively, to ponder your game plan for the next day or week and create a list of tasks that need to be completed to advance your goals. If you don't, the day or week is going to manage you, and your efficiency will be dramatically reduced. Finally, the simple activity of reviewing your day for a few minutes will consciously and subconsciously anchor your mind to the accomplishment of the day just completed if it was successful, and establish a mental commitment to make tomorrow better.

SELF-CONTROL AND SELF-DENIAL

Self-control is both a core value and a tactic of self-discipline. There is great benefit in the simple tactic of being able to force yourself to do a task (or tasks) you don't relish doing. The power of self-control is the acknowledgment of a force or reason more important than your immediate desires and a recognition your body will obey your Being and do what needs to be done, even if it is not your most favorite thing to do at the moment. Self-control is a very blunt, direct tactic of self-discipline, the value of which cannot be denied.

Self-denial is somewhat similar to self-control, and it requires the personal strength to force yourself *not* to do something that, at least superficially, you might like to do. Like self-control, it can be considered both a core value and a tactic. Self-denial is a wonderful habit that can be learned and one that is extremely beneficial to apply to accomplish any goal.

Both these tactics are among the great lessons young people learn from playing organized sports—the coach pushes you to try a little harder and, since you are doing something you are really committed to (a value, a vision and purpose), the team member is very willing to exert the extra effort that is encouraged—or even demanded by the coach. With the help of an externally imposed authority figure, the player learns the value of enforced control over self as well as the benefits of denying pleasures that don't contribute to the immediate goal.

It is interesting how all the stars line up between the sports practice analogy and the process of self-discipline: in addition to values, vision and goals, there is accountability and authority imposed on the athlete to make it easier to make the immediate task decisions and/or commit to the extra self-control or self-denial required. And, there is often peer pressure to succeed.

DON'T NEGOTIATE WITH YOURSELF

Don't negotiate with yourself on tasks necessary to advance your goals. Not all necessary tasks are particularly pleasant, but their execution is important to achieving your goals. If you allow yourself to internally negotiate whether or not you will follow through with a necessary task, you open the door to failure. You must constantly force yourself into the habit of your body following the guidance of your Being and always refuse to allow yourself to be talked out of something that has to be done. Allowing negotiation with yourself is the development of a bad habit, and the good habit is being aware of the pitfall and consistently refusing to engage in that negotiation.

DAILY TACTICS:
MORNING ROUTINE

Good morning. Let's begin our discussion of daily self-discipline tactics at the beginning of the day, when you have the opportunity to set up your day for success. Creating initial positivity sets the tone for a productive experience that will contribute to your well-being and ultimate success. Without minimizing the importance of a morning routine, I want to encourage you to adopt one that fits your personality. Make sure your routine is set up for success, not failure.

You always have the option of what to do with your mental state. The first thing in the morning is the perfect time to manage and establish your mindset for the day ahead. The framework you set for yourself will subconsciously guide you throughout the day and enable you to be positive and productive, moving yourself along your vision and toward your greater purpose in life.

There are many specific techniques for establishing a regular morning routine but, importantly, simply recognize that scheduling five to fifteen minutes for yourself at the beginning of the day is a critical component of making your life successful. Take a few minutes—right at the beginning of your day—to recognize that nothing is more important than giving this time to yourself, for the betterment of your life and the accomplishment of your life purpose. Find a quiet place—a room, your bed, a bathroom, a backyard space—where you can steal away for a short time and reflect on your Being and the day ahead of you. This time is extremely important; don't ignore it.

I suggest you start your day by acknowledging gratitude for three things in your life significant to you. Yes, there may be things less than wonderful happening in your life, but this is the time to focus on positive things, giving them power and influence on your attitude. Take a few minutes and consciously think of three things for which you are grateful. They can be people in your life, personal accomplishments, successes you have experienced, situations contributing to your well-being, or just simple niceties of living such as a comfortable bed or a warm breeze. Take stock of three good things and express gratitude for having them in your life. Appreciate your good fortune for having these things in your life and the fact that not everyone does.

Recognize the entire manifestation of your life will be in the day in front of you and ask yourself, "What can I do today to make it great?" Importantly, the answer to this question doesn't have to be earthshattering; it can simply be a positive accomplishment in the ordinary course of your day. But consciously focus on achieving that accomplishment, even if it is somewhat routine. Of course, there's nothing wrong with stretching your "make today

Chapter 13: Tactics for Task Accomplishment

great" intention, but be careful not to set the intention so high it is a recipe for failure. Another early morning question that is very positive is to ask, "How can I make today better than yesterday?" Both these practices establish wonderful mindsets to begin your days with, and thinking them will make you significantly more productive than you otherwise would be.

When you think about your life reduced to one day, why wouldn't you spend a few minutes appreciating it, organizing and planning it? Does it make any sense to just barrel down the road without any plan for success? Absolutely not. Take charge of your life by taking charge of your day, and the best time to do it is first thing in the morning. Don't let your life just happen to you by default; be sure to be the commander of your own fate, and the tactic of a quality morning routine is the place to start.

Your morning routine has to fit your personality, and you need to be mindful of not ruining your day with an unachievable routine. I will share a contrasting example of the importance of "staying in your lane," so to speak, regarding morning routines.

General Stanley McChrystal retired from the US Army after 34 years of service, and his last assignment was as the commander of all American and Coalition forces in Afghanistan. I read about McChrystal's morning routine in Tim Ferriss's great book, *Tools of Titans*.[34] I'm going to take the general's morning routine directly from Ferriss's book (because it is so detailed) and tell you this is an overwhelming standard to aspire to. Here's what retired General McChrystal does in the morning, starting his workout at home:

---

34 Tim Ferriss, *Tools of Titans: The Tactics, Routines, and Habits of Billionaires, Icons, and World-Class Performers* (New York: Houghton Mifflin Harcourt, 2016), 437–438. This is a wonderful compendium of tools, techniques, and hacks by some of the most impressive people in the world. Get it.

1. Set of push-ups to max reps
2. 100 sit-ups, 3-minute plank, 2 to 3 minutes of yoga
3. Set of push-ups to max reps
4. 50 to 100 crossover sit-ups (the first two variations combined), 2-minute plank, 2 to 3 minutes of yoga
5. Set of push-ups to max reps
6. 60 flutter kicks, followed by static hold; 1.5-minute plank; set of crunches; 1-minute plank; 2 to 3 minutes of yoga

That routine starts at 4:30 a.m., and then he goes to the gym and does four sets of pull-ups, alternated with inclined bench press and standing curls, along with a few other things.

I include this example of a morning routine for several reasons. First, we all know some people are superhuman, and they are certainly not the majority of us. I couldn't even *contemplate* doing that level of physical exercise, much less *do* it. If you could remotely accomplish something like McChrystal's routine daily, you would probably be on track to be a four-star general who is reporting daily to the White House. God bless you if you are, but let me focus on the rest of us mortals for a minute.

Your morning routine is your opportunity to set up your day, and it should include some physical exercise and some mental preparation and planning for the day ahead of you. But be realistic about this process—it has to work for you. Unless you are Stan McChrystal or Jocko Willink,[35] it doesn't have to include a thousand push-ups or the equivalent level of exercise. I do some exercise in the morning but, after listing McChrystal's routine, I am embarrassed to tell you what mine is. The important thing is I *have* a routine and I do my best not to miss it. Short as mine

---

[35] Jocko Willink is the author of *Discipline Equals Freedom* (St. Martin's Press, 2017), an entertaining and informative read with a great perspective on building self-discipline.

is, my physical exercise routine exists, and when I complete it, I have a keystone habit to check off my list of accomplishments for the day. As author Jake Knapp writes, "Starting my day with exercise gives me a big mood and energy boost throughout the day and makes me feel like I've accomplished something right off the bat."[36] I strongly encourage you to include some physical exercise—the right amount for you—in your morning routine.

Finally, it's important that you *don't* use your morning routine time for worrying about the "difficult" day ahead. This private time should be focused on positive thoughts about yourself, your capabilities, and your ability to solve any life problem presented to you. Our brains are structured to be analytical problem solvers, but part of managing your mindset is stepping away from the necessary analysis and focusing on the right side of your brain to reinforce the confidence you should have in yourself to solve the mundane problems in front of you.

STEPS TO APPLY A MORNING ROUTINE

1. Set aside five to fifteen minutes dedicated to setting the tone for a productive day.
2. Focus on three things in your life for which you are grateful.
3. Envision the completion of a necessary task to make this day great.
4. Make your morning routine fit your personality.
5. Commit to a morning routine at least five out of seven days and evaluate whether the application of the morning routine enhances your life.

---

[36] Jake Knapp, mymorningroutine.com/jake-knapp/

REVIEWING YOUR DAY AND SETTING UP TOMORROW

As with all of the tactics of self-discipline, there is no absolute right way to implement them. Contemplate all of them and try to implement the ones that work for you. In keeping with the philosophy of kaizen (constant improvement), take a few minutes at the end of each day to review your contribution and success of the day. During your review time, ask yourself: "Did I do better today than I did yesterday?" Look at the day you have just completed and compare it to the day before. It is very important *not* to beat yourself up for a negative answer to that question (and there will be many days when there will be negative answers), because asking the question sets up your mindset to do a little better the next day. And, of course, there is no rule against setting up a brief review time once or twice during your day to evaluate where you are in the process of accomplishing your goals.

In *Tools of Titans*, venture capitalist Reid Hoffman talks about spending every night setting up a problem before he goes to bed so he will subconsciously think about it during the night, then he gets up the next morning and spends an hour working on it.[37] This is an approach that obviously works for him, and it may not work for you, but it is certainly worth thinking about as a strategy for success. I would suggest the review process is almost as important as the planning process.

DAILY REVIEW EXERCISE

1. Identify a quiet moment you set aside for yourself each evening either at the end of the workday or before you retire.

---
[37] Ferriss, *Tools of Titans*, 230.

2. Ask yourself: "Did I do better today than I did yesterday?"
3. In a positive way, commend yourself for the successes of the day or, without judgment, commit to bettering yourself tomorrow.

WEEKLY COMMITMENTS

Somewhat similar to a morning routine is the practice of establishing weekly commitments you can plan and track. These commitments should consist of one goal from each of four or five areas of your life composing your core values and your vision for yourself in the medium term. Making your weekly commitments is your opportunity to think about the week ahead and plan a level of daily activity you will contribute to each of your goals. Here are some examples of weekly commitments appropriate to consider:

1. Morning exercise routine—five out of seven days
2. Three daily gratitudes—seven out of seven days
3. "Make today great" commitment—five out of seven days
4. Work on strategic business plan—one hour, four out of seven days
5. Research European travel options—one hour, two out of seven days
6. Three-mile run—three out of seven days
7. Socialize with my group—two evenings (or maybe one evening with my group and one evening with some new group)

In fairness, having seven items on your weekly commitment list is on the high side, but having weekly commitments you establish as goals for yourself, with the understanding you are going to review your success in hindsight, is an extremely effective technique for self-accomplishment. Schedule a standard time, once a week, to sit down and contemplate the week ahead and review the week just finished. I promise you this practice will increase your efficiency dramatically in the pursuit of your goals.

STEPS TO ACCOMPLISH WEEKLY COMMITMENTS

1. Select a time once a week to sit down and take stock of both the week ahead and the week past.
2. For the week ahead, review your current goals and select four or five of them from different categories (professional, school, personal, health, social, etc.), and identify a daily achievable task that can be accomplished in pursuit of those goals.
3. Prepare a daily tracking sheet similar to the example on page 154 to simply give yourself a checklist to keep track of your performance.

DAILY TRACKING SHEET

A simple daily tracking sheet is another key to productivity success. When you establish your weekly commitments to yourself, you set five or six goals you believe are important for you to accomplish during the present week, and you know

Chapter 13: Tactics for Task Accomplishment

each goal requires necessary tasks to accomplish it. A daily tracking sheet simply records those tasks and provides the incentive for you to check off their completion. The tracking sheet should be motivational, not punitive. By that I mean the sheet should make you feel the thrill of accomplishment early in your day. For example, the sheet I have in front of me today starts with my short physical exercise routine—not a particularly difficult task to accomplish and give myself emotional credit for. (It's 5:04 a.m. and my exercises are already checked off.) I have also already checked off my three gratitudes (that I thought about before I even got out of bed), and I have also checked off—but not completed—the commitment to do something to make today great. (My "make today great" thing today is a project at work I have been putting off, and my task is to simply spend about an hour looking over the file and starting to think about it.) Finally, I have my gym/pool clothes on and I am already primed to go to the gym (which really means drive my wife over there—she's a hell of a motivator for me, fortunately), so that's another "x" in the tracking sheet. Damn—just writing this shows me my tracking sheet is a little skinny. If I can check everything off by 6:00 a.m., I'd better set some loftier goals for myself. But I trust you get the point: there is definitely a benefit in carrying around a simple scorecard that keeps track of your ongoing accomplishments and helps to psychologically hold your feet to the fire. My daily tracking sheet is a simple half sheet of paper with a penciled-in grid that looks like this:

	Push-ups	Three Gratitudes	Make Today Great	Daily Exercise Routine	Business Objective
Sun.					
Mon.					
Tues.					
Wed.					
Thurs.					
Fri.					
Sat.					

QUICK REVIEW AND RESET RITUAL

Particularly if it's positive, reviewing the most recent fifteen minutes of your life can be beneficial to taking control of the next little part of your life. Take credit for the good things you've done and be sure not to compare yourself to some standard that takes away from your good feeling of present accomplishment. I suggest you use this technique if you slow down during the day and need a pick-me-up.

You have the power (and the duty) to reset your mind whenever you aren't in a positive, productive mood. You can accomplish this as follows:

    a. Stop the mental activity that isn't supporting you at the moment;

    b. Take a few deep breaths and drop into a state of relaxation;

c. Separate yourself from your negative thoughts (the meditation technique that says "you are not your thoughts");
d. Realize you are in control of the next few minutes of your life (and really nothing more) and use the "baby steps" technique;
e. Get yourself engaged in the moment. Keep your focus small and you can get into it, and;
f. Do a few very small things that advance your goals and purpose, like thinking through some tiny planning or, for me, getting up and doing something rather than thinking about something, like writing a few lines or a paragraph about something. When I do this, I am applying my guiding principle that "I am action this moment, not thought."

In summary, review the most recent ten or fifteen minutes of your life and, if you haven't been "on task," push the reset button by initially focusing your mind on what you could positively be doing for the next short period of time. Redirect yourself by undertaking a few small tasks in pursuit of your goals. The psychological benefit of this "reset ritual" can be huge. Try it; you'll see.

IDENTIFY THE TIME PERIOD THAT WORKS FOR YOU

As part of controlling your life, it is important to identify the appropriate length of time during which you can exercise control. For me, that time period is about thirty minutes. Simply stated, I can force myself to "work"—to do some task that might be less than pleasant—for about thirty minutes. If I tell myself that I am going to "work" on some task for four hours, I am usually kidding myself, and that attempted commitment will lead to failure and frustration. But I can commit to doing something for thirty minutes, and that proves to be a recipe for success for me—both practically and psychologically. In other words, I can actually accomplish a thirty-minute task (or tasks), and I enjoy the psychological benefit of accomplishment. This comes from understanding my attention span and working around it. If I am successful in my life, my epitaph should read something like: "He lived in thirty-minute chunks." Figure out the time period that works for you; be aware of it, and try to schedule your activities to fit within that time frame. Not being able to concentrate on something for hours on end isn't a failure or a weakness. It's just a reality of life. Turn it into a strength and work with it.

ORGANIZING

The tactic of organizing is such an obvious hack, it's difficult to even discuss, but we all fail at it from time to time. We can only focus our attention on one thing at a time, and it's foolish to allow our minds to be cluttered with distractions when we're trying to accomplish important tasks. So, the exercise of organizing ourselves—our days, our work spaces, our desks, our kitchens—is fundamental to making effective use of the next half hour.

Aside from current clutter, another easy trap to fall into is distracting yourself from the present moment by thinking about (or starting to do) the next task on your list. Have you ever had one of those days where you were busy as hell and, when you reflected on the day, you realized you didn't accomplish anything? Organizing the spaces around you will help to organize your focus and enable you to much more efficiently accomplish your goals.

DO TWO THINGS INSTEAD OF ONE

In a conversation several years ago, my good friend Tracy Morales matter-of-factly mentioned a practice she always applies when working in her kitchen: she never performs one task alone; she always tries to combine one little chore with another for the sake of efficiency. Similarly, she tries to never move from point A to point B without doing at least one adjacent task along the way. Since then, every time I make a move in the kitchen (or elsewhere), I try to incorporate Tracy's brilliant technique into my activity. Why get one thing out of the refrigerator when you can get two? Or, why only do X when you can easily combine it with Y and Z? The point of this very simple tactic is obvious: you get two tasks done for the price of one. Also, you get the psychological benefit of feeling smart because you're being very efficient and you're checking off two tasks from your list, even if the necessary tasks are so small they never made it to your list. This is a very minor tactic, but every little hack helps.

DOING THE NEXT BEST THING

I developed a theory about life activities in my late teens and early twenties. I would watch friends of mine sitting around complaining about their condition in life and saying things like, "I don't know what I want to do," or "I don't like where I live," and they would sit around doing nothing while they waited to figure it out. From that experience, I developed the concept of always "doing the next best thing." The concept applies to just about everything in life because it forces you to always be doing something positive instead of fantasizing about the perfect thing you should be doing. It applies to everything: jobs, school, college majors, dating, traveling, absolutely everything. Don't allow yourself to sit around doing nothing while you dream about the perfect thing to do; get off your behind and do the next best thing for the next ten minutes (or hour, or day) of your life.

This tactic also eliminates the procrastination problem of the perfection syndrome, or thinking that the next task you have to do needs to be done perfectly. It's easy to use this blocking mechanism to resist moving forward, and the "next best thing" tactic helps overcome this roadblock.

CHAPTER EXERCISE

1. Identify two or three keystone habits relevant to your goals and commit to doing each of them every day for two weeks.
2. Divide the day ahead of you into one-hour segments and frame necessary tasks into sixty-minute bites. Also be aware of the mental mindset of the next sixty seconds and try to take control of that time frame with positive, forward-thinking thoughts.

Chapter 13: Tactics for Task Accomplishment

3. Create a list of "shoulds" from your thinking about your near-term goals. Using that list, reduce each item to a list of "can-do" tasks. Referring to item #2, make the tasks doable in one-hour commitments, or less.
4. For at least one short- or medium-term goal of yours, establish a deadline within one week's time to complete the necessary tasks to accomplish the goal.
5. Consider involving a close friend or acquaintance to help you establish a time deadline to complete one or several important tasks.
6. Schedule a time when you can spend at least thirty minutes of uninterrupted time away from all distractions. Focus on a medium- to long-term goal of yours and begin to visualize every aspect of the successful completion of the goal. Where will you be? How will you feel having accomplished the achievement? Who will be with you? What will they think of your having achieved your goal? Experience the personal satisfaction of feeling the completion of the goal.
7. Be mindful of the way you are thinking of things on your task list. Be aware of the different ways (positive or negative) you can think about tasks you have to perform and the different levels of energy resulting from your prospective thinking.
8. Research and identify different time management systems and choose one that works for you. Commit to using your chosen system for two weeks to see if it enhances your productivity.
9. Commit to exercising self-control over yourself in order to perform necessary tasks. Do not allow yourself to negotiate your way out of doing what is needed.
10. Identify a private time early in the morning when you will establish your mindset for the day ahead.

11. At the end of each day, take a committed time to review the results of the day and contemplate how you will address tomorrow.
12. Design a daily tracking sheet similar to the example on page 154 and choose four or five commitments you will make for the following week. Schedule a time one week later to review your performance.
13. Be mindful of the quick review-and-reset ritual always available to you.
14. What is the ideal time period that works for your personality?
15. When you perform short, simple tasks, try to add another simple task to the activity so you can take advantage of doing two things at once.
16. Always be mindful of the "next best thing" you could fall back to and recognize that a perfection syndrome is detrimental to the incentive to move forward on your personal achievement process.

SECTION V
ROADBLOCKS TO SELF-DISCIPLINE

CHAPTER 14

THE SEVEN DEADLY SINS OF TASK AVOIDANCE
... AND WHAT THE REAL PROBLEM MIGHT BE

If you remain somewhat stuck, or if you're having difficulty moving forward on the path you think you should be on, there may still be one obstruction to be conquered. Superficially, the impediments to moving forward seem to be seven deadly sins holding us back: procrastination, perfection syndrome, distraction, interruption, busyness, simple laziness, and apathy. These insidious task-avoidance obstacles block our forward progress in the journey of personal achievement. As a quick aside, these seven aren't the only devious tricks keeping us from advancing; they are just the major ones, and they conveniently number seven.[38]

In studying the issue of task avoidance, I have become aware that a primary reason for failing to aggressively move forward is often some psychological fear either paralyzing us or making it much more difficult to advance on the path of personal achievement. You may think you are unable to advance your goals because you fall victim to the sin of procrastination or the perfection syndrome, or one of the other sins, but you may be paralyzed for some other reason. I am not a psychologist, so I am not the best person to analyze this problem,

---

[38] I will suggest some other task-avoidance tricks: lack of focus, wavering commitment to your core values, distorting your priorities, fantasy, scatterbrain, overanalysis—thinking/rethinking/rethinking—worry, uncertainty of purpose, fear of conflict, paralysis.

but I can identify the possible problem and discuss it briefly. Most importantly, you should be aware of the possible psychological roadblock to your advancement and work to understand and overcome it. Sometimes a psychological barrier works hand in hand with the task-avoidance tricks so that one might mask the other.

The challenge is figuring out what the particular problem might be. Is it fear of failure? Fear of success? Fear of angering someone? Fear of one-upping someone? Fear of changing your present situation? Fear of not doing it well enough? I'm sure there are a hundred psychological roadblocks chilling us into inaction (or diverted action), but the important thing is to be in touch with the possibility when you find yourself stymied from progress, and then work to understand the reason and what is necessary to overcome it. I have identified common fears and listed a handful of them for your consideration at the end of the chapter.

If you're following the affirmative steps of a personal achievement process and implementing the strategies and tactics of self-discipline and you're still having trouble executing the necessary tasks to achieve your goals, I would suggest you are a candidate for some internal reflection or a consultation with someone who can explore the possibility there may be some psychological basis for your inertia. If, after learning the strategies and tactics of self-discipline, you still can't get moving, there might be something emotional holding you back. Don't fret, by the way; there's nothing particularly wrong with that possible fact, but recognizing that it might be your reality is at least half of the battle of overcoming it.

First and foremost, the barriers to your progress might be all the opposites of knowing your core values; having a life vision that follows your core values and is in alignment with them; developing SMART goals pursuant to, and in alignment with,

Chapter 14: The Seven Deadly Sins of Task Avoidance ... and what the real problem might be

your values and vision; failing to task and time-adjust your goals; and failing to apply intelligent strategies and tactics to accomplish your tasks. These aren't psychological barriers; they are simply failures to follow the rules of mastering self-discipline. The failure to implement any of those things, or some combination of them, creates an obstacle to your ability to exercise self-discipline to perform the necessary tasks to achieve your goals.

Another possible roadblock to moving forward is overanalyzing your situation and your path forward. One of the themes I have discussed throughout this book is the fact that you only "own" the next minute of your mental capacity and maybe the next hour or so of your physical capacity. Anything beyond those two immediate time frames is fantasy and not reality. So if you spend your mental energy analyzing what is wrong with your plan or thinking about what might not work instead of forcing yourself to move forward on your necessary tasks, you are wasting valuable productive time and investing your energy in a negative way on something outside of your mental or physical control. By engaging in those activities—worry, stressing out about the future, lamenting some past action—you are sabotaging your achievement process and not capitalizing on the techniques you know how to implement. Take a look inward: something emotional may be keeping you from achieving your goals.

One remedy to overcome these insidious inhibitors is a well-crafted personal achievement process with properly tasked and time-adjusted goals so the seven deadly sins of task avoidance don't creep in and divert you from achieving your goals. The task-avoidance sins may be the result of not having a clear personal achievement plan—meaning you don't know where you really want to go—or they may result from a conflicted achievement plan, which is the same thing: you're unsure of where you want to go. Another possibility is that your inertia is based on some psychological insecurity about where you should be going: fear of failure, fear of success, fear of displeasing someone, fear of conflict, or many other possibilities. It's your responsibility to figure it out and determine your own way to move forward.

With the admonition that there might be more to your inertia than the obstacle of the seven deadly sins, I will discuss each of the "sins."

PROCRASTINATION

Procrastination is the practice of avoiding the execution of a necessary task in favor of doing a less-important replacement task or simply doing nothing. Procrastination provides an immediate emotional satisfaction from doing the replacement task as well as a superficial pleasure from avoiding the undesirable necessary task. It is the mortal sin of the seven deadly sins because it is often the manifestation of one or more of the other task-avoidance tricks. Procrastination is a complicated and treacherous practice deserving of a detailed discussion, and it is the subject of Chapter 15.

PERFECTIONISM

In psychology, perfectionism is a personality trait characterized by a person's striving for flawlessness and setting high performance standards, accompanied by critical self-evaluations and concerns regarding others' evaluations.[39] It is a trait with both positive and negative

---
39 Joachim Stoeber and Julian H. Childs, "The Assessment of Self-Oriented and Socially Prescribed

aspects.[40] In its negative form, perfectionism drives people to attempt to achieve unattainable ideals or unrealistic goals. Its victims can indefinitely procrastinate doing a necessary task by continually reviewing the task in their minds instead of executing it, because they are not satisfied they'll do it perfectly enough. If you envision perfection in your necessary tasks, you raise a high level of concern over making mistakes, and it becomes psychologically intimidating to actually do the tasks. The perfection syndrome is a terrible task-avoidance pattern, causing procrastination, inertia and a corresponding feeling of disappointment leading to a level of depression. If you are hindered from progress by perfectionism, first recognize you're doing it—you're "in your head" obsessing about how to make the next step of your necessary tasks better and more perfect—and then realize you're sabotaging your way forward. Perfectionism can be overcome by employing some of the tactics of task accomplishment in Chapter 13, particularly the tasking of goals into baby steps and time-adjusting them into short time segments. Finally, recognizing the quote attributed to Voltaire, "The perfect is the enemy of the good," we should all realize there is little value in perfectionism.

DISTRACTION

Distraction is a convenient trick to play on yourself, or with yourself, to avoid doing necessary tasks. Your mind can always find something supposedly more important than the thing you ought to be doing,

---

Perfectionism: Subscales Make a Difference," *Journal of Personality Assessment* 92, no. 6 (2010): 577–585, doi: 10.1080/00223891.2010.-513306. PMID 20954059. This quotation is taken from Wikipedia.

40 Hongfei Yang and Joachim Stoeber, "The Physical Appearance Perfectionism Scale: Development and Preliminary Validation," *Journal of Psychopathology and Behavioral Assessment* 34, no. 1 (2012): 69–83, doi: 10.1007/s10862-011-92607. Quotation taken from Wikipedia. In contrast with its negative implications, perfectionism can be a positive personality trait that helps motivate people to reach their goals and enjoy the fruits of their achievement. Its positive attributes are not the subject of this chapter.

especially if there is some psychological reason preventing you from moving forward. It's easy for your brain to be sidetracked and then be immediately placated by filling the void with other less important tasks. Since distraction is something that usually happens in the moment, the tactics to help avoid it are planning, prioritizing, organizing and scheduling. When you review your performance at the end of your day, be mindful of whether you allowed yourself to be the victim of distraction. If so, create a plan to deal with the issue the next day.

INTERRUPTION

How long has it been since you had a day so cluttered with interruptions you didn't get anything meaningful done? For most of us, unfortunately, the phenomenon happens more often than we would like to admit. We are barraged with phone calls, emails, requests and casual conversations that appear to demand our attention and distract us from the tasks at hand. The shortsighted excuse for this deadly sin is it isn't caused by us; it's caused by others, and there's nothing we can do about it. Well, that just isn't an acceptable reason to allow interruptions to constantly interfere with progress toward achieving your goals. It is absolutely critical to claim your self-worth and take control of your time, not allowing dozens of interruptions to interfere with your productivity. Evaluate your professional situation in relation to your core values and restructure your calendar to provide uninterrupted time to execute necessary tasks. The most successful professionals schedule interruption time so it doesn't conflict with productivity. There's nothing wrong with saying something like "I routinely return emails or phone calls after 2:00 p.m." You are ultimately responsible for your own destiny and you can't allow your tombstone to read: "He never accomplished anything significant—he was constantly interrupted with unimportant stuff."

BUSYNESS

Constant busyness is a form of task avoidance. It results from the failure to prioritize and schedule necessary tasks. It is a destructive practice controlling our time, diverting our attention, and keeping us from realizing our goals. The failure to prioritize and schedule your professional time causes you to constantly be too busy, too distracted to get to the important goals you have established for yourself. Step back and evaluate your professional situation. What is important versus what is just clutter? You have to be the judge. Busyness is a condition that you are in charge of, and it undermines your effective productive time, diluting your efforts to achieve your goals.

FANTASY

You can't negate the value of dreaming and fantasy, but you should be aware of the point at which fantasy overtakes one's ability to productively move forward. There comes a point in task avoidance when you know you are using your imagination as an excuse to put off doing the necessary tasks ahead of you. That is the time to take stock and fall back on the tactics of task accomplishment that move you forward. When you are trading productive work time for idle dreaming, step back from your thoughts, task your goals into manageable bites, and get to work. You will feel much better accomplishing something than thinking about it.

WORRY

Worrying is a trap of your thinking process that occasionally has some importance but is usually used as a mental excuse for inaction. Nine times out of ten, the thing you are worrying about doesn't materialize in the way you are imagining it will, and your worry is effectively a waste of time. It is analogous to stressing out about next Thursday on Monday morning. If there is a reason to plan for some contingency next Thursday on this Monday, then turn the contingency plan into a task you can do now to ameliorate your concern about the upcoming event. Don't waste current valuable mental energy with unproductive worry about things that might not happen.

LAZINESS AND APATHY

I'm going to group these two sins together for my brief discussion of them. Seriously? What is your problem? Don't you care? Have you lost sight of your goals? Isn't this important to you anymore? Was it ever important? What is important to you? Where do you want to go with your life? I don't think I can help you much with this one. If you're this far along understanding the personal achievement process and the strategies and tactics of self-discipline, these sins probably aren't problems for you, but if they are, you can probably figure out how to kick yourself in the ass to get moving. Sorry I had to mention them.

Chapter 14: The Seven Deadly Sins of Task Avoidance ... and what the real problem might be

PARALYSIS

If you just can't make yourself move forward, you are probably being blocked by some emotional fear. You have learned the tools to execute a personal achievement process and there should be no reason why you can't implement them. Why can't you get off the dime and move forward? What is causing you to freeze? I can only suggest some of the following emotional roadblocks may apply to your situation. Take a look inward and ask yourself if you can conquer the problems by yourself or if you should seek outside support. Following are some of the things that might be inhibiting you, in layman's terms.

EMOTIONAL ROADBLOCKS THAT MIGHT BE HOLDING YOU BACK

1. Fear of failure
2. Fear of success
3. Fear of being judged
4. Fear of emotional pain
5. Fear of embarrassment
6. Fear of being abandoned or being alone
7. Fear of rejection
8. Fear of expressing your true feelings
9. Fear of intimacy
10. Fear of the unknown
11. Fear of loss
12. Fear of dying

WISH I HADN'T COMMITTED

One final example of task avoidance is the feeling that comes over you when you just don't want to move forward on something on your to-do list. This feeling can result from getting drawn into doing something because you told someone you would do it and then discovering you wish you hadn't. The reason you can't get motivated to proceed is that the commitment isn't pursuant to a core value or desire you have. It's because you told somebody you'd do it, and that isn't enough motivation to get you to do the necessary tasks to accomplish the goal. Because you have committed, you might conclude you just have to do it and get it over with. Alternatively, you might consider renegotiating the commitment. Over the years, I have learned to evaluate whether I really want to commit to someone and to have the courage to say no to requests I don't have the time or energy to enthusiastically fulfill.

In conclusion, take a self-reflective look into what might be holding you back from aggressively moving forward toward your goals. With your knowledge of the strategies and tactics of self-discipline, you should be able to navigate your personal achievement process to create a way forward. Look deeply into what might be holding you back and consider seeking some other perspectives (professional guidance or opinions of close confidants) to help you move forward.

CHAPTER 15

PROCRASTINATION

Almost everyone does it a little—or a lot—and we hate the feelings procrastination causes in us. We also hate the inefficiency that putting off a project causes and, when we finally complete the task, we feel bad because we could have done it so much better if we hadn't stalled on moving it forward. Procrastination is an insidious practice because it works against us in so many ways. Understanding the psychology of procrastination is very helpful as we try to conquer it.

Charlotte Lieberman describes procrastination as a perfect example of *present bias*, "our hard-wired tendency to prioritize short-term needs ahead of long-term ones."[41] We often think of it as a character defect or a simple lack of motivation to get the job done. Oftentimes, procrastination is the habit fueling the apparent lack of self-discipline to accomplish the tasks necessary to achieve our goals. But Lieberman points out that "procrastination isn't a unique character flaw or a mysterious curse on your ability to manage time, but a way of coping with challenging emotions and negative moods induced by certain tasks—boredom, anxiety, insecurity, frustration, resentment, self-doubt and more."

The study of procrastination leads us to conclude that in a reverse-bargain way, procrastination is a trading of the emotion

---

41 Charlotte Lieberman, "Why You Procrastinate (It Has Nothing to Do with Self-Control)," *New York Times*, March 25, 2019.

of the present for the future. There is some reason why you don't want to do a necessary task in front of you; some psychological resistance—possibly some fear—that enables or tricks your mind into thinking you would rather replace the necessary task with some other task. The other task may be worthwhile, or it may be either nothing or busy work. You get a certain immediate satisfaction from the current replacement task as well as a superficial pleasure from not doing the undesirable, necessary task. However, you have deferred some pain or frustration into the future when you will feel bad or frustrated from not doing the thing you should have done in the first place. You also become burdened with the ongoing headache of having the deferred task on your to-do list.

In short, procrastination creates an immediate superficial joy and a long-term deeper frustration. It's easy to fall into because of what psychologists call the temporal disjunction between our present and future selves. In simple English, that means it's easy to trade immediate gratification by avoiding something unpleasant in exchange for the future consequences of our inaction. Procrastination is scientifically defined as the self-regulatory failure of not exerting the self-control necessary for task engagement.[42]

So, how do we beat procrastination? By understanding the psychology of procrastination, you become aware it isn't a character defect or a simple lack of effort. If you realize there is an emotional barrier causing you to resist doing the aversive tasks you should be doing, you can begin to identify the negative feelings contributing to your resistance. Are you expe-

---

42 Fuschia Sirois and Timothy Pychyl, "Procrastination and the Priority of Short-Term Mood Regulation: Consequences for Future Self," *Social and Personality Psychology Compass* 7, no. 2 (February 2013): 115–127, DOI: 10.1111/spc3.12011.

Chapter 15: Procrastination

riencing a fear of success? Fear of failure? The overwhelming feeling that the mountain is just too high to climb? There may be reasons you are putting off doing the necessary tasks in front of you, and you should reflect on those reasons to try to overcome the inertia.

The pain of procrastination is a future suffering difficult to emotionally appreciate in the present tense. The act of procrastination is temporal disjunction—we give in to feel good now—meaning we will pay the price later.[43]

There's no absolute quick fix for the habit of procrastination, but understanding its demoralizing effects is a good starting place in working to overcome it. It is helpful to focus on your core values and your vision—the medium-term goals in your life—and realize you are sacrificing them for a cheap sugar high of immediate satisfaction. Arguably, the current satisfaction is superficial in the grand scheme of things, and it is not remotely worth the trade-off of sacrificing your medium-term goals for it.

And, of course, on a more basic level, you can implement many of the tactics of self-discipline to overcome your short-term desire to sell out and not do what you know you should do. Let's be honest: there's definitely some value to just sucking it up, buckling down and doing what you need to do for the next thirty or sixty minutes. Be aware procrastination is robbing you of implementing your core values and the well-thought-out vision you have for your life. Fight it as hard as you can and don't give in; take control of your life and your destiny.

---

[43] Dianne Tice and Ellen Bratslavsky, "Giving In to Feel Good: The Place of Emotion Regulation in the Context of General Self-Control," *Psychological Inquiry* 11, no. 3 (July 2000): 149–159.

CHAPTER EXERCISES
(they're not foolproof, only a start)

1. Take a few minutes and contemplate why you are resisting doing the task you know you need to do.
2. Recognize there is an emotional resistance to moving forward, not a rational one.
3. Write a short plan to accomplish the task you are avoiding.
4. Ask yourself: "What is the next action I would take if I were going to do the undesirable task, even though I am not?"
5. Analyze the avoided task and break it into three to five subparts. Identify the time and energy it will take to complete (or begin) one of the subparts.
6. Organize the next thirty minutes of your life to include a simple, preliminary part of the task you are avoiding.
7. Create a short time period you will identify for doing the undesirable task.
8. On your daily planner, schedule fifteen to thirty minutes—later in the day—to address the undesirable task.
9. Forgive yourself for your immediate procrastination and create a reward you will give yourself for embarking on the task ahead.
10. Don't wait to be in the mood to undertake the avoided task. Get started, and you will find the mood of achievement follows.
11. Generally, make the undesirable task as easy as possible for yourself. Remove as many obstacles from doing the task as you possibly can.

Chapter 15: Procrastination

12. Fast-forward and recognize how good you will feel as you embark on and complete the task you are trying to avoid.
13. Also recognize you will not avoid the task—it will just hang over your head and suck the energy out of you until you finally do it. So the act of procrastination makes the task many times more difficult than it already is.
14. Just plain suck it up and do it.

SECTION VI

LIVING A DISCIPLINED LIFE

Mastering Self-Discipline

CHAPTER 16

SELF-DISCIPLINE IS LEADERSHIP:
THE CHARACTER, COHESION AND DIRECTION OF THE GROUP

The key to successful leadership today is influence, not authority.
—Ken Blanchard

In our professional lives, most of us function as part of a larger organization of people attempting to pursue some business-type objective.[44] It may be a small business, a Fortune 500 corporation, a government entity or a professional practice providing services to clients. Unless you are a sole proprietor who has no employees, you probably function as part of a team of people pursuing a goal.

The concepts and techniques of personal self-discipline apply to our professional activities, with the primary difference being that the principles apply to the entire business group, not just the individual. A professional achievement process is similar to a personal achievement process, providing a foundation for the core values of the organization and establishing the basis for the goals of the entity. An organization's foundation is embod-

---

44 This includes government, education and nonprofit organizations.

ied in its mission statement, its strategic plan and its business plan. These documents comprise the "soul" of the organization and they provide the foundational basis for the direction of the members of the group.

At the foundational level, a company's mission statement is comparable to an individual's "Finding Your Soul" discussed in Chapter 3. The mission statement indicates a greater purpose for the existence of the organization. Core values and life vision are concepts equivalent to a company's strategic plan and business plan. Similar to an individual's foundation for self-discipline, it is essential for the organization to have its goals and beliefs carefully determined and reduced to written statements communicated to all members of the group. These fundamental commitments create the foundational principles guiding the organization and consequently all of its members.

Every organization has a professional achievement process in place, whether it realizes it or not. The question is whether it is an effective, affirmative process or a lackadaisical one. If a company doesn't have a positive, affirmative plan in place reduced to writing and communicated to its entire team, inertia will assure very little happens. The poor foundation of the ineffective plan will result in

Chapter 16: Self-Discipline Is Leadership: The Character, Cohesion and Direction of the Group

unfocused effort on the part of team members and the outcome will be exactly what you would logically expect: nothing special.

Being part of a team means all members have the responsibility to determine the way in which they fit into the larger organization, and if they don't, that fact should raise concern. It's essential to find a professional organization with which you are compatible, meaning your core values are aligned with the entity's values. Synergy exists when individual members of a team are in synch with the organization, and synergy benefits everyone. Self-disciplined individuals are aware of their core values, the importance of acting in alignment with those values, and the necessity of working in a professional environment compatible with their values and vision. It is untenable for a disciplined person to try to fit into an organization that *isn't* compatible with his or her values.

Assuming alignment between the individual and the professional organization, the exercise of an individual's self-discipline has significant benefits to the entity. When individuals understand the personal achievement process described in this book, their ability to implement the necessary tasks to achieve corporate goals is dramatically enhanced. Because task accomplishment for corporate goals is no different from personal goals, the same strategies and tactics apply. In the corporate setting, there is the benefit of both management pressure and peer pressure to apply the tactics of deadlines, accountability, planning, scheduling and regular review. To enforce tactics, every team member has the benefit of being both a follower and a leader. There is no doubt having some type of authoritative structure to respond to (as a responsible member of a team) can have motivational benefits in keeping all participants on track. In this regard, every team member is a follower, being accountable to the team for their individual actions. But every team member is also a leader, requiring accountability from other members of the team.

A team member develops leadership skills by exercising self-discipline in the organization, helping to develop the goals aligned with the entity's strategic and business plan, and then tasking and time-adjusting those goals so they can be achieved by all members of the group. Because the same techniques of task accomplishment apply to a professional achievement plan, the challenge is to involve all members of the group in the completion of necessary tasks. An individual excels within a group by getting to know the team, helping co-workers and taking initiative. When an individual in a group understands and exercises more self-discipline, there is a positive effect on everyone else and the individual is credited with a leadership role in the group.

The important role of individual team members as leaders cannot be overstated. The challenges of evolving personal self-discipline into corporate discipline don't usually result from failure of corporate leadership at the top, but rather from team leadership throughout the organization. And team leadership is implicitly much more democratic and more influential than it is authoritarian. The principles of self-discipline contribute to making every organization member a leader by giving him or her the skills of task accomplishment and goal achievement. The exercise of individual self-discipline is contagious and it increases the character, cohesion and direction of the entire group.

Leadership skills are exercised constantly between members of a group by means of one person acting with character and integrity, explicitly setting an example for other members of the group. If an individual is exercising self-discipline in her personal and professional life, her own character is significantly enhanced

Chapter 16: Self-Discipline Is Leadership: The Character, Cohesion and Direction of the Group

by the commitment to her values and the execution of tasks in pursuit of her goals. Character—good or bad—is contagious, and a group member's character will spread to her peers through example. Your disciplined actions are observed by others, and the effect of your actions is the transmission of the principles of self-discipline to the entire group. In its application in a business or organizational setting, self-discipline comprises leadership, a concept existing to some degree in every human interaction.

The more people in an organization who understand and implement self-discipline, the more democratic leadership exists and expands in the company. Two kids on a soccer team working hard are observed by two of their teammates, and their commitment to self-betterment and goal achievement is infectious. This is the principle of "a rising tide lifts all boats," and it applies to any individual working within a group.

Leadership has become more informal in recent times. It is frequently one's strength of character that exemplifies leadership among professionals, not a formal rank. Gone are the days where the bosses were segregated from the employees, referred to as "Mr." or "Ms.," and required to eat in the executive dining hall. Now everyone is on a first-name basis and the formalities of authoritative leadership have fallen by the wayside. Leadership is exercised at every level in an organization through each person's relationships with their team members. It doesn't matter if there are only two people on an assignment; one or both of them can and should be exercising leadership skills. Others see what a person is doing, and they are inclined to model that behavior. A leader's job is to focus on his own personal achievement process and exercise of self-discipline, and the effects of personal discipline will be observed and modeled by the people around him.

Leaders are made, not born. It takes practice, and if you look hard enough and get creative, you'll notice plenty of hidden opportunities all around you to strengthen your leadership muscle. Every person reading this book is or will be in a management or leadership role in a professional organization at some point in time, and everyone—at every level—has management and leadership responsibilities. Leadership can be implemented in every nook and cranny of the organization; it doesn't just come from one person at the top of the pyramid. Leadership means doing the right thing and setting an example for those around you; it's about stepping up and becoming the kind of person others aspire to be. Your exercise of self-discipline in all your professional activities results in bettering yourself and the organization in which you work.

CHAPTER 17

THE RESULTS OF SELF-DISCIPLINE
(FREEDOM, HAPPINESS AND MORE)

The exercise of self-discipline seems difficult at first. The notion you have to force yourself to do things you don't want to do seems intolerable. Why would someone want to do that? You're killing yourself with struggle and effort to do tasks that aren't desirable. Superficially, most people would rather just enjoy their lives and not be bothered with the aggravation of a long to-do list dominating their time.

As you develop the practice of more easily performing necessary tasks, you begin to realize the pleasure flowing from achieving your well-thought-out goals. The exercise of self-discipline results in a more enjoyable level of engagement in the necessary tasks required to achieve your goals. Self-discipline creates contentment because nothing makes you happier than realizing your life vision.

The irony is this: exercising what appears to be the difficult undertaking of self-discipline to accomplish necessary tasks puts you in a state of contentment because you are doing things in pursuit of your goals. If your goals are aligned with your core values, performing the necessary tasks to achieve them is no longer a chore but a pleasing experience. You are thrilled to execute these tasks because you are achieving your goals, even though it may be only one tiny step at a time. When you are comfortably moving along your life vision path, you experience a deep emotional satisfaction that is simply incomparable.

The exercise of self-discipline creates emotional freedom from the burden of carrying around the baggage of having to do X, Y and Z that so many people are saddled with. If we spent half as much time *doing* our lives as we spend thinking about doing our lives, stressing about doing our lives, or fretting about what we're not doing in our lives, life would be much simpler, more free and much happier. The mastery of self-discipline focuses on doing our lives and living our lives, rather than thinking about our lives. There is certainly a place for thinking about living, but actually living is much more gratifying. When you have mastered self-discipline, you are no longer thinking about living, you are living.

Feel free to email brian@brianbrinig.com with any comments, observations or struggles you have with mastering self-discipline. I look forward to hearing from you.

APPENDIX
Self-Discipline Tool Kit

This tool kit is your minute-to-minute guide to gain control of your actions after you understand the personal achievement process encompassing self-discipline. It really works.

1. Get control of your head
    a. For only 30 seconds
    b. Get out of the past (lament); get out of the future (worry)
2. Come to the present
    a. It's the only life you ever have
    b. Acknowledge and realize this fact
3. Recognize you are in control
    a. "My Being controls my body"
4. Determine goals that are important to you
    a. Be certain your goals are Specific, Measurable, Achievable, Relevant, and Time-sensitive
5. Task your goals into manageable short-term steps
6. Time-adjust your goals over a defined period of time so the necessary tasks can be accomplished in the near-term future
7. Commit to some action now, for the next 15–30 minutes
    a. "I use this moment to move ahead of the curve"
8. Adopt an immediate positive attitude toward the task in front of you
9. Reaffirm your belief in your ability to accomplish the task
10. Visualize the completion of the necessary task
11. Fall back on your guiding principles

12. Act now. If necessary, do the next best thing
13. Reward yourself for action.

ABOUT THE AUTHOR

Brian Peter Brinig is both a lawyer and a CPA, the founder and managing director of a major financial consulting firm in San Diego and an Adjunct Professor at the University of San Diego School of Law. He is a graduate of Georgetown University School of Business and a veteran of the United States Marine Corps, having served a twelve-month tour in Vietnam. He has written three technical books for lawyers and financial professionals, and in recent years, his professional interest has been the art of self-discipline for individuals and businesses. He is a nationally recognized continuing education speaker to universities, professional organizations and corporations, and he has qualified as an economic expert witness in more than one hundred jury trials in federal and state courts across the United States. He and his wife, Lisa, live in San Diego, California.

ACKNOWLEDGMENT

Last but by no means least, I want to acknowledge the enormous contribution to this book by Ms. Jill Thiry, my professional life coach for the year of drafting this work. Many of the strategies and tactics of self-discipline in this book are the same methods Jill helped enforce on me during the somewhat arduous writing process. Without her support, *Mastering Self-Discipline: A Thoughtful Approach Gets Better Results* would not exist. A sincere thank you, Jill.

www.ingramcontent.com/pod-product-compliance
Lightning Source LLC
Chambersburg PA
CBHW070302010526
44108CB00039B/1575